WOOLLY BEAR KNITS

WOOLLY BEAR KNITS

20 patterns for sweaters, mittens, toys and more – all with adorable bear designs

MELINDA COSS

St. Martin's Press
New York

This book is dedicated to
Spencer Bear of Cambridge

Paddington Bear © Paddington and Company Ltd 1989;
Licensed by Copyrights

Rupert Bear © Express Newspapers plc

LIBRARY OF CONGRESS CATALOG CARD NUMBER:
89–42846

ISBN 0–312–02355–3

Produced by the Justin Knowles Publishing Group,
9 Colleton Crescent, Exeter, EX2 4BY, UK

First published 1989 by Aurum Press Limited
under the title *Teddy Knits*.

First U.S. Edition

10 9 8 7 6 5 4 3 2 1

Printed and bound in Italy by Amilcare Pizzi s.p.a.

CONTENTS

ABBREVIATIONS

alt	alternate
beg	begin(ning)
C6B	slip 3 sts onto a cable needle and hold at back, k3, k3 from cable needle
C6F	slip 3 sts onto a cable needle and hold at front, k3, k3 from cable needle
C8B	slip 4 sts onto a cable needle and hold at back, k4, k4 from cable needle
C8F	slip 4 sts onto a cable needle and hold at front, k4, k4 from cable needle
cont	continue/continuing
dec	decrease/decreasing
in	inch(es)
inc	increase/increasing
k	knit
k1b	knit stitch through back loop
MB	make small bobble (*see* Techniques, page 9)
MBL	make large bobble
p	purl
psso	pass slipped stitch over
rep	repeat
RS	right side(s)
sl	slip
ssk	slip 1 stitch, knit 1 stitch, pass slipped stitch over
st(s)	stitch(es)
st st	stockinette stitch
tbl	through back of loop(s)
tog	together
WS	wrong side(s)
yo	place yarn over right-hand needle from back to front to make another st
yrn	wrap yarn around right-hand needle from front to back to make another stitch

TECHNIQUES

READING THE CHARTS

Throughout the book explanatory charts show the color designs charted out, with stitch symbols added where necessary. Each square represents one stitch across, i.e., horizontally, and one row up, i.e., vertically. The charts should be used in conjunction with the written instructions, which will tell you where and when to incorporate them. Any colors required or symbols used will be explained in the pattern. Always assume that you are working in stockinette stitch unless otherwise instructed.

If you are not experienced in the use of charts, remember that when you look at the flat page you are simply looking at a graphic representation of the right side of your piece of work, i.e., the smooth side of stockinette stitch. For this reason, wherever possible, the charts begin with a right side (RS) row so that you can see exactly what is going on as you knit. Knit rows are worked from right to left and purl rows from left to right.

FAIRISLE

The technique of color knitting called "fairisle" is often confused with the traditional style of color knitting that originated in the Fair Isles and took its name from those islands. Knitting instructions that call for the fairisle method do not necessarily produce a small-motifed repetitive pattern similar to that sported by the Prince of Wales in the Twenties—far from it, as can be seen from some of the patterns in this book.

The method referred to as fairisle knitting is when two colors are used across a row, with the one not in use being carried at the back of the work until it is next required. This is normally done by dropping one color and picking up the other, using the right hand. If you are lucky enough to have mastered both the "English" and "Continental" methods of knitting, the yarns being used may be held simultaneously, one in the left hand, the other in the right hand. The instructions below, however, are limited to

the more standard one-handed method and give the three alternative methods of dealing with the yarn not in use.

Stranding

Stranding is the term used to describe the technique by which the yarn not in use is simply left hanging at the back of the work until it is next needed. The yarn in use is then dropped and the carried yarn taken up, ready for use. This means that the strand, or "float", thus produced on the wrong side of the work has a direct pull on the stitches either side of it.

The wrong side of the work, showing stranding at the correct gauge.

It is essential to leave a float long enough to span this gap without pulling the stitches out of shape and to allow the stitches in front of it to stretch and not to pucker on the right side of the work. It is preferable to go to the other extreme and leave a small loop at the back of the work rather than pull the float too tightly.

If the gap to be bridged by the float is wide, the strands produced may easily be caught and pulled when the garment is put on or taken off. This problem may be remedied by catching the floats down with a few stitches on the wrong side of the work at the finishing stage.

Weaving

With this method the yarn being carried is looped over or under the working yarn on every stitch, creating an up and down woven effect on the wrong side of the work. Since the knitter does not have to gauge the length of the floats, many people find that this is the easiest method of ensuring an even, accurate tension. Weaving does increase the chances of the carried color showing through on to the right side of the

The wrong side of weaving, showing the up and down path of the carried yarn.

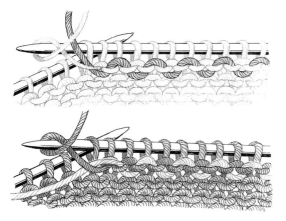

background, keep the motif gauge as close to the background gauge as possible. If there is a great difference, the motif stitches will distort the image.

INTARSIA

Intarsia is the term used for the technique of color knitting whereby each area of color is worked using a separate ball of yarn, rather than carrying yarns from one area to another as in the fairisle technique. Any design that involves large blocks of isolated color that are not going to be repeated along a row or required again a few rows later, should be worked in this way.

There are no limitations to the number of colors that may be used on any one row other than those imposed by lack of patience and/or dexterity. Avoid getting into a tangle with too many separate balls of yarn hanging from the back of the work and remember that every time a new ball of yarn is introduced and broken off after use, two extra ends are produced that will have to be secured at the end of the day. When ends are left, always make sure that they are long enough to thread up so that they may be

work, however, and it tends to produce a far denser fabric, which is not always desirable when a thick fiber is being used.

Stranding and weaving
Combining the two methods of stranding and weaving is invariably the most practical solution to the problem of working perfect fairisle. Most designs will have color areas that will vary in the number of stitches. If the gap between areas of the same color is only a few stitches, then stranding will suffice, but if the float produced will be too long, weave the carried yarn in every few stitches. Should you be unsure about the length of float to leave, slip your fingers under one. If you succeed with ease, the float is too long.

Stranding and weaving worked too tightly.

The most difficult aspect of fairisle knitting is getting the gauge correct. This does not depend on the stitch size so much as on the way you treat the carried yarn. This is why, when working an all-over fairisle, you should always knit a gauge sample in fairisle, not in main color stockinette stitch, as the weaving or stranding will greatly affect the finished measurement of the stitches. The most important rule to remember is that *the yarn being carried must be woven or stranded loosely enough to have the same degree of "give" as the knitting itself.* Unless this is achieved, the resulting fabric will have no elasticity whatsoever and, in extreme examples, very tight floats will buckle the stitches so that they lie badly on the right side of the work.

If you are using the fairisle technique to work a color motif on a single-color

If you are using the intarsia method, twist the yarns firmly together when you change colors.

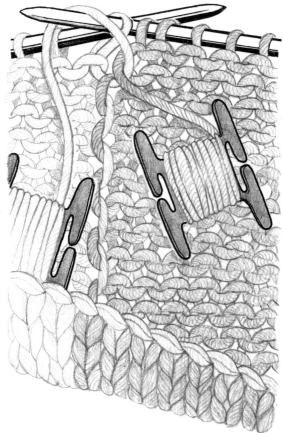

properly fastened with a pointed tapestry needle. Do this very carefully through the backs of the worked stitches to avoid distorting the design on the right side of the work. The ends that are left should never be knotted because they will make the wrong side of the work look extremely unsightly and they will invariably work themselves loose and create problems at a later stage.

If only a few large, regular areas of color are being worked, avoid tangling the wool by laying the different balls of yarn on a table in front of you or keep them separate in individual jam jars or shoe-boxes. However, this requires careful turning at the end of every row so that the various strands do not become twisted.

The easiest method is to use small bobbins that hold each yarn separately and that hang at the back of the work. Such bobbins are available at most large yarn stores or they may be made at home out of stiff cardboard. They come in a variety of shapes, but all have a narrow slit in them that keeps the wound yarn in place but allows the knitter to unwind a controlled amount as and when required. When winding yarn on to a bobbin, try to wind sufficient to complete an entire area of color, but don't overwind, as heavy bobbins may pull stitches out of shape.

When you change color from one stitch to another, it is essential that you twist the yarns around one another before dropping the old color and working the first stitch in the new color. This prevents a hole from forming. If it is not done, there is no strand to connect the last stitch worked in color "A" to the first stitch worked in color "B". This twisting should also be done quite firmly to prevent a gap from appearing after the work has settled.

MAKING A BOBBLE

There are numerous variations on the theme of bobble making, but in this book we have used just two, which, for ease of identification, we have called large and small, abbreviated as MBL and MB. If worked on a right side (RS) row, the bobble will hang on the right side, if worked on a wrong side (WS) row, push it through on to the right side.

Large bobble
1. When the MBL position on the row has

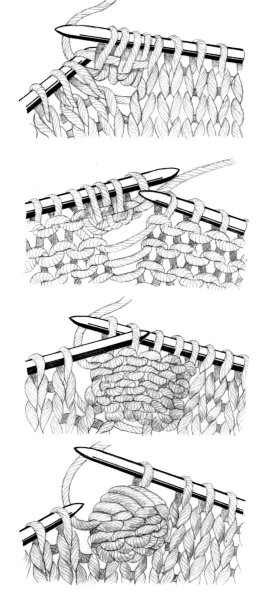

The four steps in making a bobble are illustrated here. If you work a bobble on the wrong side, push it through to the right side of your work.

been reached, make 5 stitches out of the next one by knitting into its front, then its back, front, back and front again before slipping it off the LH needle.
2. Turn the work and knit these 5 stitches only.
3. Turn the work, purl 5 and repeat the last 2 rows.
4. Using the point of the left-hand needle, lift the bobble stitches, in order, over the first one on the right-hand needle, i.e., 2nd, 3rd, 4th and 5th, so that one stitch remains.

After completing the bobble, the work may continue as normal, the single stitch having been restored to its original position on the row.

Small bobble

To make a small bobble, as for the Rupert design, k 3 sts from 1, turn, k3, turn, sl 1, k2 tog, psso.

CABLES

A basic cable is simply a twist in the knitted fabric caused by working a small number of stitches out of sequence every few rows. This is done by slipping the stitches on to a needle and leaving them at the front or the back of the work while the next stitches on the left-hand needle are worked. The held stitches are then worked normally. The cable, worked in stockinette stitch, will always be flanked by a few reversed stockinette stitches to give it definition. Since it does involve a twist, however, cabled fabric will always have a tighter gauge than one worked in plain stockinette stitch, so take extra care when working a gauge sample.

Cable needles are very short and double-pointed. Some have a little kink in them to help keep the stitches in place while others are being worked. Use one that is a similar size to the needles being used for the main work and take care not to stretch or twist the stitches when moving them from needle to needle.

On the right side of the work, if the stitches are held to the front, the cable will cross from the right to the left. If the stitches are held at the back of the work, the cable will twist from the left to the right.

Front cross cable

1. (RS): work to the six stitches that are to be cabled. Slip the next three stitches on the left-hand needle onto the cable needle and leave them hanging at the front of the work.
2. Knit the next three stitches on the left-hand needle as normal.
3. Knit the three held stitches off the cable needle.

Repeat this twist wherever indicated in the instructions.

The same basic technique may be used to move a single stitch across a background of stockinette stitch at a diagonal, rather than form a cable that moves up the work vertically.

Where the abbreviation cb2 is used, the first stitch is slipped on to the cable needle and left at the back of the work while the next stitch is knitted. The held stitch is then knitted off the cable needle. Cf2 is the same but with the cable needle left at the front of the work. On purl rows the abbreviations pcb2 and pcf2 are used to denote the same movement but in which the stitches are purled rather than knitted. In this way a continuous criss-cross line is formed.

SEAMS

After achieving the correct gauge, the final sewing up of your knitting is the most important technique to master. It can make or break a garment, however carefully it may have been knitted. This is why the finishing instructions after every set of knitting instructions should be followed exactly, especially to the type of seam to be used and the order in which the seams are to be worked.

Before starting any piece of work, always leave an end of yarn long enough to complete a substantial section, if not the whole length, of the eventual seam. After working a couple of rows, wind this up and pin it to the work to keep it out of the way. If required, also leave a sizable end when the work has been completed. This saves having to join in new ends that may well work loose, especially at stress points.

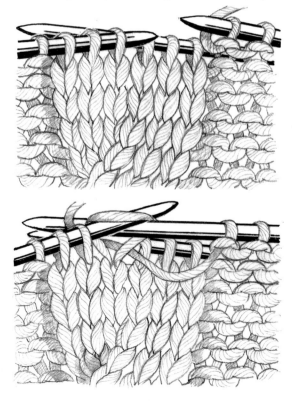

The front cross cable.

10

The secret of perfect-looking seams is uniformity and regularity of stitch. When joining two pieces that have been worked in the same stitch, they should be joined row for row, and all work should be pinned first to ensure an even distribution of fabrics. When joining work that has a design on both pieces, take great care to match the colors, changing the color you are using to sew the seam where necessary.

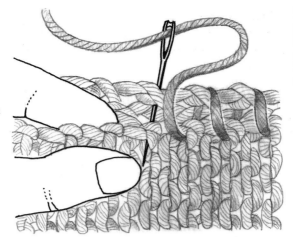

The drawings show (above) how you should hold the knitting to work a flat seam and (below) how your work will look on the right side.

Backstitch

Pin the two pieces of work together, right sides facing, making sure that the edges are absolutely flush. Always leave as narrow a seam allowance as possible to reduce unnecessary bulk. It is essential that the line of backstitches is kept straight, using the lines of the knitted stitches as a guide. All the stitches should be identical in length, one starting immediately after the previous one has finished. On the side of the work facing you, the stitches should form a continuous, straight line. If the seam is starting at the very edge of the work, close the edges with an overcast stitch as shown. Now work the backstitch as follows:

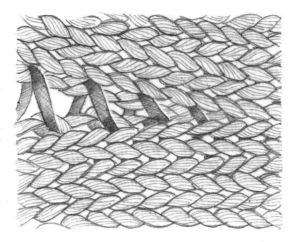

1. Make a running stitch (maximum length ½in), through both thicknesses of work.
2. Put the needle back into the work in exactly the same spot as before and make another running stitch twice as long.
3. Put the needle back into the work adjacent to the point where the previous stitch ended. Make another stitch the same length.

Keep repeating step 3 until the last stitch, which needs to be half as long to fill in the final gap left at the end of the seam.

By keeping the stitch line straight and by pulling the yarn fairly firmly after each stitch, no gaps should appear when the work is opened out and the seam pulled apart.

This seam is suitable for lightweight yarns or when an untidy selvedge has been worked.

Flat seam

This seam is a slight contradiction in terms since its working involves an overcast stitch action, but when the work is opened out it will do so completely and lie quite flat, unlike a backstitched seam.

Use a blunt-ended tapestry needle to avoid splitting the knitted stitches. Pin both pieces right sides together and hold the work as shown. The needle is placed through the very edge stitch on the back piece and then through the very edge stitch on the front piece. The yarn is pulled through and the action repeated, with the needle being placed through exactly the same part of each stitch every time. Always work through the edge stitch only. By taking in more than this, a lumpy, untidy seam that will never lie flat will be produced.

When two pieces of stockinette stitch are to be joined with a flat seam, do not work any special selvedge such as knitting every edge stitch. Just work the edge stitches normally but as tightly as possible, using only the tip of your needle. When you come to work the seam, place the needle behind the knots of the edge stitches and not the looser strands that run between the knots, since these will not provide a firm enough base for the seam, which will appear gappy when opened out.

Flat seams are essential for heavy-weight yarns where a backstitch would create far too much bulk. They should also be used for attaching buttonbands, collars and so forth, where flatness and neatness are essential.

Borders, waistbands, cuffs and any other part of a garment where the edge of the seam will be visible should be joined with a flat seam, even if the remainder of the garment is to have a backstitched seam. Start with a flat seam until the rib/border is complete and then change over to a backstitch, taking in a tiny seam allowance at first and then smoothly widening it without making a sudden inroad into the work.

EMBROIDERY

To achieve the detail necessary for the facial features of some of the bears incorporated into the garments, simple embroidery stitches have been added after the knitting has been completed. You may find it helpful to sketch roughly on to the fabric, using tailor's chalk or lines of very small pins, the position and outline of the embroidery.

Satin stitch
Satin stitch is used to "fill-in" areas such as

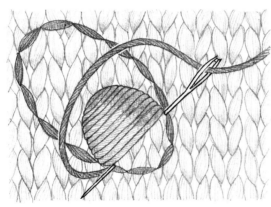

eyes. It is formed by working straight stitches, very close to one another, over the length of the area to be covered.

Backstitch
Outlines are worked in backstitch, which should be worked in exactly the same way as the stitch used for seams (see page 11). When you are working a curve, try to make very small stitches to ensure a continuous line.

Chain stitch
Bring needle up through back of work and back down at starting point and up again under loop. Pull through ready for the next stitch.

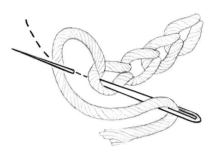

French knots
Push the needle through the knitting, wind wool twice around the needle, pull wool through and insert needle back at starting point.

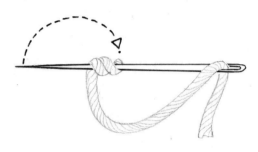

Daisy stitch
Bring needle up through back of work and back down at starting point and up again under and over loop. Bring needle up again at starting point and repeat chains in a circle to form a daisy.

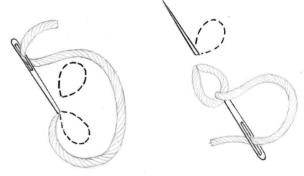

Keep the loops of chain stitch to the same tension and work in smooth curves.

French knots are used to make the centers of flowers.

When you embroider facial features such as eyes use satin stitch for solid areas and backstitch for outlines.

When you work daisy stitch, make sure that the loops are evenly sized and spaced.

Swiss darning

This is the most straightforward method of embroidery that may be worked on knitted fabrics since it exactly duplicates knitted stitches. For this reason Swiss darning is sometimes called "duplicate stitch". By following the path of the knitted stitch with a contrasting color, it is possible to create a variety of designs that have the appearance of being worked as a complicated fairisle, although they have, more simply, been added afterwards. For knitters who are not too confident with color techniques, this is a very useful adjunct to their knitting skills.

When Swiss darning, always use a yarn of the same thickness as the knitting so that it will cover the stitch beneath it but not create an embossed effect. Use a blunt-ended tapestry needle to avoid splitting the knitted stitches as you embroider. The tension of the embroidered stitches must be kept exactly the same as the work that is providing the base so that they sit properly and do not pucker the work. The tension is regulated by how tightly the embroidery yarn is pulled through the work at each stage. Take great care when joining in and securing yarn ends on the wrong side of the work so that the stitches in the area do not become distorted.

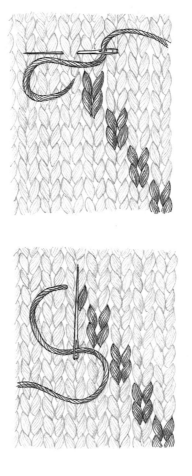

When you use Swiss darning to complete a motif, make sure that you use yarn of the same thickness as the knitting and that you follow the path of the knitted stitches.

MAKING A POMPON

Cut out two cardboard circles approx 4in in diameter with holes in the center as shown. Hold the 2 circles together and, using the main color wound into a ball small enough to pass through the center hole, wind the yarn around and around, keeping the strands close together. Cont wrapping the yarn around, working as many layers as you can from the remaining yarn and before the center hole becomes too small for the ball of

yarn to pass through.
Using sharp nail scissors, slip a blade between the two layers of cardboard and cut around the circumference of the circle.
Slip a length of yarn between the two layers and around the center of what will become the pompon.
Pull tight and knot the yarn before pulling the two pieces of cardboard away (cut them if this proves difficult).
Shake and trim the pompon into shape.

Materials
Wendy Miami – white:
250gm; red: 200gm;
yellow: 100gm; green and
turquoise: less than 50gm
of each. Approximately
26¾in of ¾in wide elastic.
Scrap of black cotton for
embroidery.

Needles
One pair of No.3 and one
pair of No.5 needles; one
No.3, 36in circular needle.

Gauge
Using No.5 needles and
measured over st st, 20 sts
and 28 rows = 4in square.

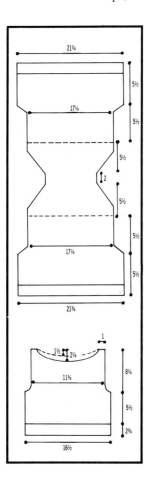

The chart opposite
should be followed to
complete the top (*see*
pages 16–17).

This fun beach outfit is worked using the
intarsia method (*see* Techniques, page 8).
The pattern is worked to fit chest/hip sizes
32/35¾in.

PANTS

Using No.5 needles and white, cast on
110 sts. Work in k2, p2 rib for 4 rows. Begin

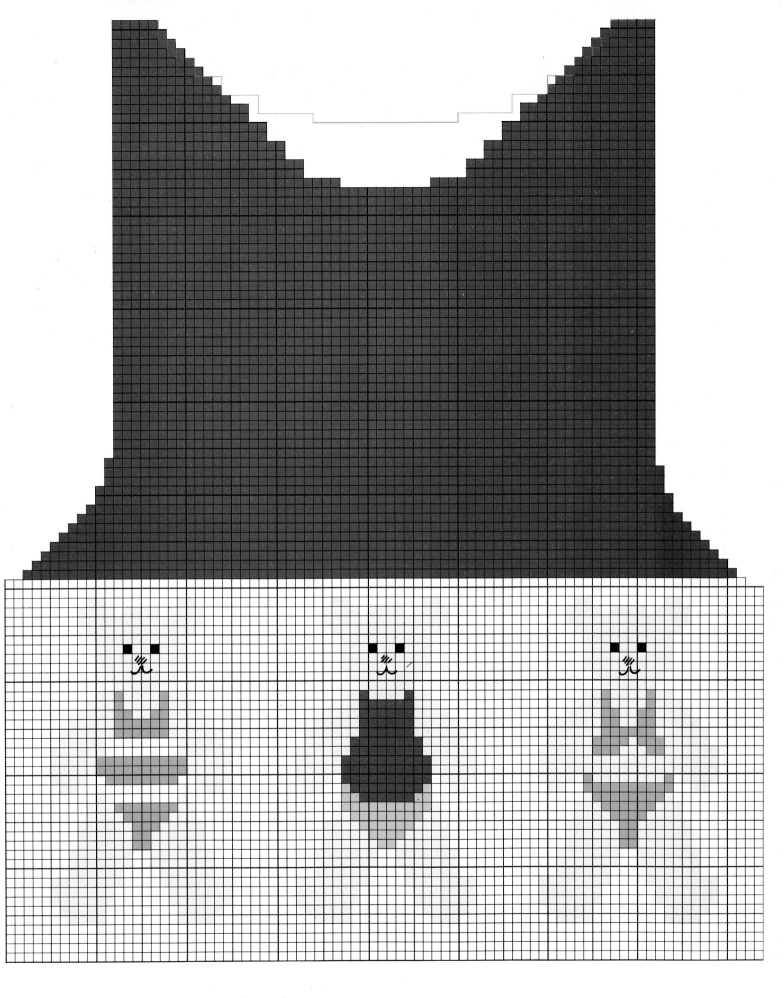

Incorporate this chart into the pants as described below.

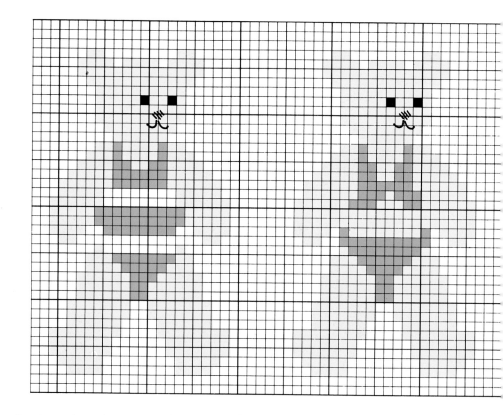

working from the chart above in st st until it is complete.

Change to No.3 needles and red. Next row: k2, k2 tog, *k3, k2 tog,* rep from * to * to last st, k1 (88 sts). Work in k2, p2 rib for 5½in ending with a RS row.

Change to No.5 needles and white and, starting with a k row, work in st st for 10 rows. Dec 7 sts at beg of next 2 rows, 6 sts at beg of next 2 rows, 4 sts at beg of next 2 rows and 3 sts at beg of the following 2 rows. Dec 2 sts at beg of next 4 rows and dec 1 st at each end of the next 6 rows. Then dec 1 st at each end of the next 6 alt rows (16 sts). Work 9 rows even. Dec 1 st at each end of the next row. Work 15 rows even, inc 1 st at beg of the next row (16 sts). Inc 1 st at each end of the following 4th row, 1 st at each end of the next 2 following 3rd rows, then the 12 following alt rows (46 sts). Cont by inc 1 st at each end of every row until you have 88 sts. Work 10 rows even.

Change to No.3 needles and red and work in k2, p2 rib for 5½in.

Change to No.5 needles and white. K1, *inc into next st,* k3, inc into next st. Rep from * to * until 2 sts remain, k2. Turn the chart upside down and work until it is complete. K2, p2 rib for 4 rows. Bind off.

Finishing
With RS together, join ribbed section with a flat seam and use a narrow backstitch on the skirt and pants. This will ensure that no seams show when the rib is folded.

Pants rib
With RS facing and using No.3 circular needle, pick up and k 124 sts around leg edge. Work in k2, p2 rib for 3 rows. Bind off loosely in ribbing.

TOP

Front
Using No.3 needles and red, cast on 84 sts. Work in k2, p2 rib for 2¾in.
Change to No.5 needles and white and begin working from the chart on page 15 in st st until it is complete. Change to red. **Shape armhole:** bind off 2 sts at beg of next 2 rows, then dec 1 st at each end of every row 8 times. Dec 1 st at each end of the next alt row and 1 st at each end of the following 3rd row*. Cont to work even to neck shaping. Next row: k25, slip remaining sts onto a stitch holder and work on this side of the neck only. Keeping armhole edge even, bind off 4 sts at beg of the next row, 2 sts at neck edge on the next 4 alt rows, then 1 st at neck edge on the next 8 rows. Work 1 row, bind off. Slip center 10 sts onto a spare needle,

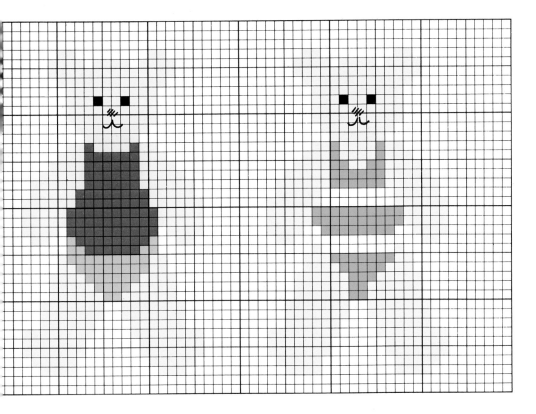

rejoin yarn at neck edge and shape other side of neck to match.

Back
Work as for front to *. Cont to work even to back neck shaping. K22, leave remaining sts on a spare needle, work on this side of neck only. Bind off 6 sts at beg of the next row, 4 sts at beg of the next alt row and 3 sts at beg of the next alt row. Bind off 2 sts at beg of the next alt row, then 1 st at neck edge on the next 2 rows. Work 1 row. Bind off. Slip center 16 sts onto a spare needle, rejoin yarn at neck edge and shape other side to match. Join shoulder seams.

Neckband
Using No.3 circular needle and red, pick up 100 sts evenly around the neck. Work in k2, p2 rib for 1¼in. Bind off.

Armhole ribs
Using No.3 circular needle and red, pick up 86 sts evenly around armhole. Work in k2, p2 rib for ¾in. Bind off loosely in ribbing.

Finishing
Join side seams using a narrow backstitch. Fold down skirt so that the red band is folded in half, inserting elastic to fit. Sew along bottom of red band through two thicknesses. Embroider facial details.

LITTLE BEARS WOMEN'S CARDIGAN

Materials

Wendy Family Choice
4-ply – forest (244) (A):
350gm; red (242) (B) and
gold (267): 50gm of each.
Wendy Ascot 4-ply –
autumn gold (412): 50gm.
8 small pearl buttons.

Needles

One pair of No.2 and one
pair of No.4 needles.

Gauge

Using No.4 needles and
measured over st st, 28 sts
and 28 rows = 4in square.
Ribs worked on No.2
needles.

This Forties-style, crew-necked fitted
cardigan is worked using the fairisle method
(*see* Techniques, page 7).

Back

Using No.2 needles and A, cast on 122 sts.
Work in k1, p1 rib for 4in, inc 16 sts evenly

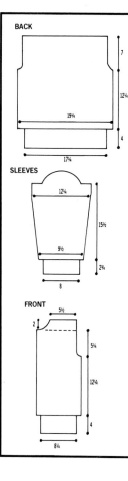

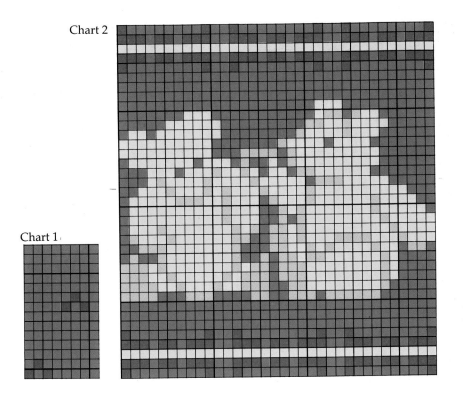

Chart 2

Chart 1

Chart 2 should be followed for the front and back of both the cardigan and the child's slipover, and for the sleeves of the cardigan.

Chart 1 should be incorporated into the front, back and sleeves of the cardigan as described on this page and on page 21, and into the front and back of the child's slipover, as described on pages 22–23.

across last row of rib (138 sts). Work 2 rows in st st in base color only, begin working from chart 1, setting it up as follows: next row: k1(A), *k5(A), k1(B), k1(A), k1(B). Rep from * to last st, k1(A). Next row: p1(A), *p1(A), p1(B), p6(A). Rep from * to last st, p1(A). Using A, work in st st for 5 rows. Next row: p1(A), *p4(A), p1(B), p1(A), p1(B), p1(A). Rep from * to last st, p1(A). Next row: k1(A), *k2(A), k1(B), k5(A). Rep from * to last st, k1(A). Using base color only, work 5 rows in st st, then begin working from chart 2, setting it up as follows: k1(A), work from chart repeating to last st, k1(A). Work the chart in this position until it is complete. Using base color only, work in st st for 3 rows, return to chart 1 and continue to work from this chart in pattern (established as previously) until the back is complete. *At the same time*, when work measures 16in from start, **shape armholes:** bind off 5 sts at beg of the next 2 rows, dec 1 st at each end of every row on the next 5 rows (118 sts). Cont working even in pattern until work measures 23¼in. Leave sts on a spare needle.

Right front
Using No.2 needles and A, cast on 58 sts. Work in k1, p1 rib for 4in, inc 10 sts evenly across last row of rib.
Change to No.4 needles and work 2 rows of st st in A. Begin working from chart 1,

setting it up as follows: row 1: k2(A), *k5(A), k1(B), k1(A), k1(B). Rep from * to the end of row. Row 2: p1(A), p1(B), p6(A), rep from beg to last 2 sts, p2(A). Using A, work 5 rows in st st. Next row: p4(A), p1(B), p1(A), p1(B). Rep to last 2 sts, p2(A). Next row: k2(A), *k2(A), k1(B), k5(A), rep from * to end of row. Using A, work 5 rows in st st, then begin working from chart 2 which repeats exactly twice across the row. Work until the chart is complete. Using A, work 3 rows in st st. Return to chart 1 and continue to work from this chart in pattern (established as previously) until front is complete. *At the same time*, when work measures 16in from beg (ending with a RS row), **shape armholes:** bind off 5 sts at beg of the next row, then dec 1 st at this edge on the next 5 rows (58 sts). Work even for 30 rows in pattern. Next row (RS): **shape neck:** keeping in pattern, bind off 5 sts, work to end of row. Dec 1 st at neck edge on every row until 38 sts remain. Work even until front matches back. Leave sts on a spare needle.

Left front
Work as for right front reversing shaping.

Sleeves (Make 2)
Using No.2 needles and A, cast on 57 sts and work in k1, p1 rib for 2¾in, inc 11 sts evenly

across last row of rib (68 sts). Change to No.4 needles and work 2 rows in st st, then begin working charts in sequence and set up as for right front. *At the same time*, keeping in pattern (and working extra sts on chart 2 in A only), inc 1 st at each end of every 15th row until you have 87 sts. Work even until sleeve measures 18in.

Shape sleeve cap. Bind off 5 sts at beg of next 2 rows. Dec 1 st at each end of every row until 65 sts remain. Dec 1 st at each end of every alt row until 33 sts remain. Bind off 4 sts at beg of the next 4 rows. Bind off remaining sts.

Front bands

Using No.2 needles and A, cast on 10 sts and work in k1, p1 rib until the band fits from the bottom of the waistband to the front edge of the neck when slightly stretched. Leave sts on a safety-pin. Place a pin to mark the first button position, 5 rows up from the cast-on edge. Mark 6 more button positions evenly up the band, making allowance for the 8th to be worked on the neckband. Work buttonhole band to correspond to marked positions for buttons as follows: rib 4, bind off 2, rib 4. On the return row, cast on 2 sts over those previously bound off. When buttonhole band matches button band, leave sts on a safety-pin.

Neckband

Knit both shoulder seams tog, leaving center 45 sts on a spare needle. Using No.2 needles and A, rib the right-hand band sts onto needle and, with RS of work facing, knit up 26 sts down right side of neck. K across back neck sts, then knit up 26 sts down left side of neck and rib the left-hand band sts (117 sts). Work in k1, p1 rib for 3 rows. Work buttonhole to correspond with others. Rib 2 more rows. Bind off in ribbing.

Shoulder pads (Make 2)

Using No.4 needles and 2 strands of main color yarn, cast on 2 sts. Work in garter st (knit every row) inc 1 st at each end of every row until you have 26 sts. Work even for 1½in. Bind off.

Finishing

Pin bands to fronts and attach with a flat seam. Join side and sleeve seams with flat seams over the ribs and a narrow backstitch over the pattern. Set the sleeves in last, distributing the sleeve cap evenly around the armhole. Attach buttons and shoulder pads.

LITTLE BEARS CHILD'S SLIPOVER

Materials
Wendy Family Choice
4-ply – red (242) (A):
200gm; forest (244) (B)
and gold (267): 50gm of
each; Wendy Ascot 4-ply
– autumn gold (412):
50gm.

Needles
One pair of No.2 and one
pair of No.4 needles.

Gauge
Using No.4 needles and
measured over st st, 28 sts
and 28 rows = 4in square.
Ribs worked on No.2
needles.

The graphs for this
pattern are on page 19.

A smart fairisle slipover to match mom's
cardigan. The pattern is written in three
sizes to fit children aged 4–5, 6–7 and 8–9
years.

Back
Using No.2 needles and A, cast on
83/97/111 sts.
Row 1: k1, *p1, k1, rep from * to end.

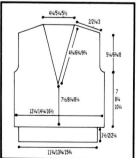

Row 2: p1, *k1, p1, rep from * to end.
Repeat these 2 rows until the work measures 1½/2/2½in, inc 3/5/7 sts evenly across last row of rib (86/102/118 sts).
Change to No.4 needles and work 2 rows in st st starting with a knit row.
Next row: begin working from chart 2 as follows: Size 1: k1 in A, knit from point on chart as indicated, repeat complete chart to last stitch, k1 in A. Size 2: work from first stitch of chart, repeat to end. Size 3: work from point on chart as indicated, repeat to end. Work chart in this position until it is complete. Work three rows in st st in A only. Next row (RS): begin working from chart 1, repeat across row. Cont following this chart until the back is complete. *At the same time,* when work measures 8¾/10¼/11¾in, **shape armholes**: next row (RS): bind off 4 sts at beg of next 2 rows, ** then dec 1 st at each end of every row until 68/80/96 sts remain. Work 1 row, then dec 1 st at each end of the next and every alt row until 60/70/82 sts remain. Work even in pattern until back measures 13¾/17/20½in ending with a purl row.
Shape shoulders: bind off 7/9/11 sts at beg of the next 2 rows, then 7/8/10 sts at beg of the following 2 rows. Leave remaining 32/36/40 sts on a spare needle.

Front

Work as for back to **. Dec 1 st at each end of every row until 70/82/98 sts remain. Cont shaping armhole as for back and, *at the same time*, **shape neck**. Next row (RS): k2 tog, k31/37/45, k2 tog, turn and leave remaining sts on a spare needle. Cont on these 33/39/47 sts for the first side and work 1 row. Dec 1 st at each end of next and every alt row until 25/29/33 sts remain. Dec 1 st at neck edge only on every alt row until 17/26/31 sts

remain, then on every following 3rd row until 14/17/21 sts remain. Work even until front matches back to beg of shoulder shaping, ending with a WS row.
Shape shoulder: bind off 7/9/11 sts at beg of next row. Work 1 row. Bind off remaining 7/8/10 sts.
With RS facing, join yarn to remaining sts. K2 tog, k to last 2 sts. K2 tog. Work to match other side, reversing shaping. Join right shoulder seam.

Neckband

Using No.2 needles, A and with RS facing, pick up and knit 39/49/63 sts down left side of neck, pick up loop at center of "V" and knit into back of it (mark this stitch with a colored thread). Pick up and knit 39/49/63 sts up right side of neck, then k32/36/40 sts from back (111/135/167 sts).
Row 1 (WS): k1, *p1, k1, rep from * to within 2 sts of marked st. P2 tog, p1, p2 tog tbl, k1. **P1, k1, rep from ** to end.
Row 2: *p1, k1, rep from * to within 2 sts of marked st. P2 tog, k1, p2 tog tbl. **K1, p1, rep from ** to end. Repeat these 2 rows twice more, then repeat first row once more. Bind off evenly in rib, dec as before.
Join left shoulder seam and neck border.

Armbands

Using No.2 needles, A and with RS facing, pick up and knit 83/105/133 sts evenly around each armhole. Starting with a second row, work in rib as for back for 7 rows. Bind off evenly in ribbing.

Finishing

Press work lightly on the wrong side. Join side seams using a flat seam. Join armband seams.

DANCING TEDDIES MOHAIR SWEATER

Materials
Wendy Soft Touch – blue (67): 450gm; white (54): 100gm; sable (62): 50gm. Approx 1¼yds of ¼in wide satin ribbon.

Needles
One pair of No.7 and one pair of No.9 needles.

Gauge
Using No.9 needles and measured over st st, 16 sts and 20 rows = 4in square. Ribs worked on No.7 needles.

This long-line fluffy sweater is covered in dancing teddies.

Front
Using No.7 needles and main color, cast on 86 sts. K1, p1 rib for 6in inc 14 sts evenly across last row of rib (100 sts). Change to No.9 needles and cont following chart to **neck shaping**: next row: k38, bind off center 24 sts, k38. Working on this last set of sts only, dec 1 st at neck edge on every row 7 times (31 sts). K4 rows in st st and leave

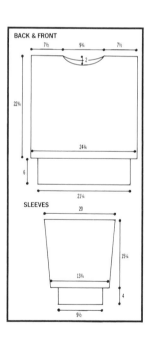

Follow the chart opposite to complete the front and the back of the sweater; the dotted lines indicate the areas to be incorporated into the sleeves (*see* page 27).

Chart 1

Chart 2

remaining sts on a spare needle. Rejoin yarn at inner edge and shape other side of neck to match. Leave shoulder sts on a spare needle.

Back
Work as for front to where shaping for back neck is indicated on chart. K33, leave center 34 sts on a holder, k33. Working on this side of neck only, dec 1 st at neck edge on next 2 rows. Work 3 rows even and leave remaining sts on a spare needle. Return to other side of neck, rejoin yarn at inner edge. Repeat shaping leaving remaining shoulder sts on a spare needle.
With RS of back and front together, knit up the shoulder seams.

Right sleeve
Using No.7 needles and main color, cast on 38 sts. K1, p1 rib for 4in, inc 18 sts evenly across last row of rib (56 sts).
Change to No.9 needles and, starting with a k row, work in st st, inc 1 st at each end of the 3rd row and the 12 following 6th rows (82 sts). *At the same time*, when 10 rows of st st have been worked, set up chart as follows: k13, k first row of chart 2. K to end in main color. Row 2: p13 in main color,

p 2nd row of chart. P to end in main color. Cont working chart in this position until it is complete. Cont shaping as before until you have 82 sts. Work 2 rows. Bind off loosely.

Left sleeve
Work as for right sleeve but use chart 1 and do not place it until 36 rows of st st have been worked – i.e., row 37: k17 in main color, k first row of chart 1, k17 in main color. Row 38: p17, p 2nd row of chart 1, p17. Cont shaping as before until chart is complete and you have 82 sts on your needle. Work 2 rows. Bind off loosely.

Neckband
Using No.7 needles and main color, pick up 92 sts evenly around the neck. Work in k1, p1 rib for 10 rows. Bind off loosely. Turn neckband to wrong side and slip st bound-off edge to pick-up edge.

Finishing
Join sleeves to sweater, join side and sleeve seams using flat seams throughout. Embroider eyes, nose and mouth on teddies where indicated. Tie small bow of ribbon, stitch into place under bear's chin.

GO EAT SOMEONE ELSE'S PORRIDGE

Materials
Wendy Ascot DK wool –
blue (937): 350gm; jade
(940): 200gm; black (423):
300gm; nut kernel (11),
chestnut (13), snowfall
(400), red poinsettia (426),
walnut (434) and crock of
gold (939), or colors to
match chart: less than
50gm of each.

Needles
One pair of No.4 and one
pair of No.5 needles.

Gauge
Using No.5 needles and
measured over st st, 24 sts
and 30 rows = 4in square.
Ribs worked on No.4
needles.

A new slant to an old story – this oversized
sweater will fit both men and women. It is
worked in double-knitting wool using the
intarsia method (*see* Techniques, page 8).

The chart opposite
should be followed to
complete the front of the
sweater.

Incorporate this chart into
the back of the sweater.

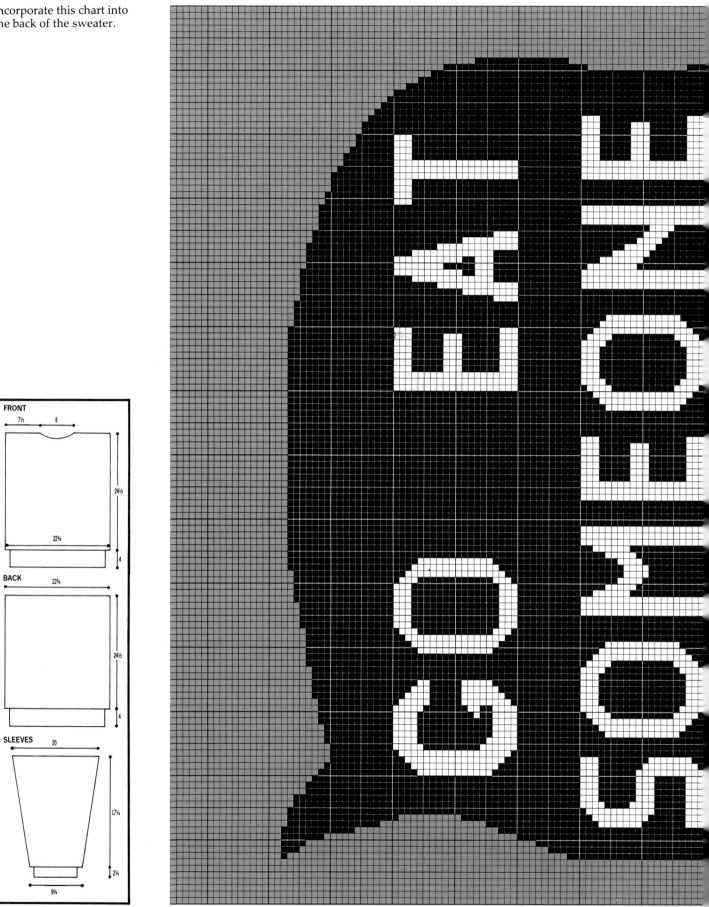

FRONT

7½   8

24½

22¾

4

BACK   22¾

24½

4

SLEEVES   20

17¼

2¼

9¾

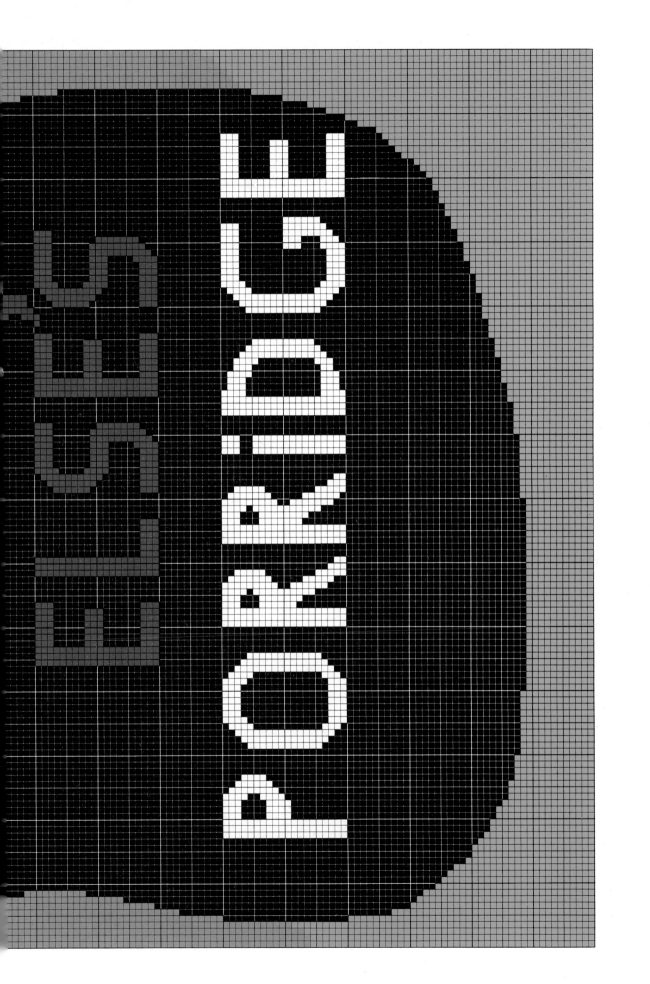

Front

Using No.4 needles and black, cast on 126 sts. Work in k1, p1 rib for 4in, inc 14 sts evenly across last row of rib (140 sts). Using No.9 needles and jade, begin following chart for front in st st to neck shaping. Next row (RS): k57, place these sts on a spare needle. Slip center 26 sts onto a stitch holder, rejoin yarn, k57. Working on this last set of sts only, dec 1 st at neck edge on the next 11 alt rows. Work 8 rows even, slip remaining 46 sts onto a spare needle. Repeat for other side.

Back

Work as for front following chart for back (eliminating neck shaping) until it is complete. Place a marker on the 46th st at each end for shoulder. Leave sts on a spare needle.

Sleeves (Make 2)

Using No.4 needles and black, cast on 56 sts and work in k1, p1 rib for 2¼in. Inc 4 sts evenly across last row of rib (60 sts). Change to No.5 needles and cont in st st inc 1 st at each end of every 4th row until you have 124 sts. Work even until sleeve measures 19¾in (including rib). Bind off loosely.

Neckband

Knit one shoulder seam together. Using No.4 needles and blue, pick up and knit the 48 sts held for center back, 30 sts down one side of front, 26 sts held for center front and 30 sts up other side of front (134 sts). Work in k1, p1 rib for 2¼in. Bind off.

Finishing

Knit second shoulder seam together. Turn neckband to wrong side and slip stitch bound-off edge to pick-up edge. Join sleeves to sweater, then join sleeve and body seams using a flat seam. Embroider mouth in black using backstitch.

Collar

Using No.4 needles, cast on 168 sts. Work in k1, p1 rib for 5¼in, bind off. Sew collar to inside of neck (starting and ending at center front).

USEFUL TEDDIES

Materials
Odd amounts of brightly colored yarn in 4-ply or DK. A piece of medium-weight cardboard. A craft knife. Rubber-based adhesive for pasting fabric to paper.

Needles
One pair of No.4 needles.

Gauge
For once this doesn't matter, just take care to knit as evenly as possible.

Here are several ways to use up your odd amounts of yarn. In addition to these special charts, the individual teddies from the Snowball Sleeping-bag (*see* page 61) have also been used.

TEDDY GREETINGS CARDS

Select the chart and color of your choice and cast on the number of stitches required.

Work 2 rows of plain knitting in st st, then complete the chart. Work 2 more rows in main color, then bind off. Steam press your completed work on the wrong side.
Place your square of knitting on the sheet of cardboard and with a ruler, pencil a square around it to the size you would like your card to be, allowing at least 1¼in all round. Cut the cardboard to the same height as the square and three times the width (with the teddy in the middle). Fold the card inwards so that the right-hand edge meets the left

The charts opposite can be incorporated into greeting cards or even used to adorn a plain sweater.

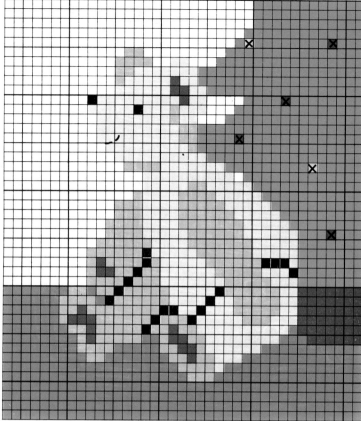

side of the center square. Then fold the left edge in to meet the right side of the center square and make firm creases down both edges. Open the card up and, using the craft knife, cut a square to match the size of your knitting in between the two creases. Turn the card over and place your teddy in the center of one of the outer squares taking care to glue it evenly. Put more glue on the surrounding card and fold this back to the center pressing it down firmly.

EMBROIDERED SWEATER

Brighten up a plain sweater by Swiss darning it with the motif of your choice. The sweater in the photograph was knitted to the basic squeaky pattern with the teddy embroidered with small amounts of DK wool. For Swiss darning (duplicate stitch) instructions, *see* Techniques, page 13.

EMBROIDERED CARDIGAN

Materials
Wendy Ascot DK wool – ecru (401): 400gm. Wendy Family Choice DK wool – red (242), green (916), yellow (267) and blue (217): 50gm of each. A scrap of black. 8 "ball-shaped" buttons.

Needles
One pair of No.6 needles; a medium-sized crochet hook; a sharp darning-needle.

Gauge
Using No.6 needles and measured over st st, 24 sts and 30 rows = 4in square.

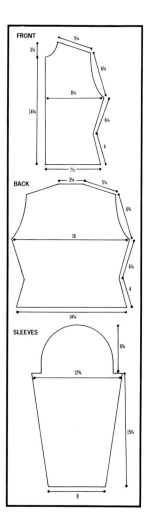

A Forties-style cable cardigan embroidered with teddies and flowers, worked in double-knitting wool.

Left front
Using No.6 needles and main color, cast on 45 sts.

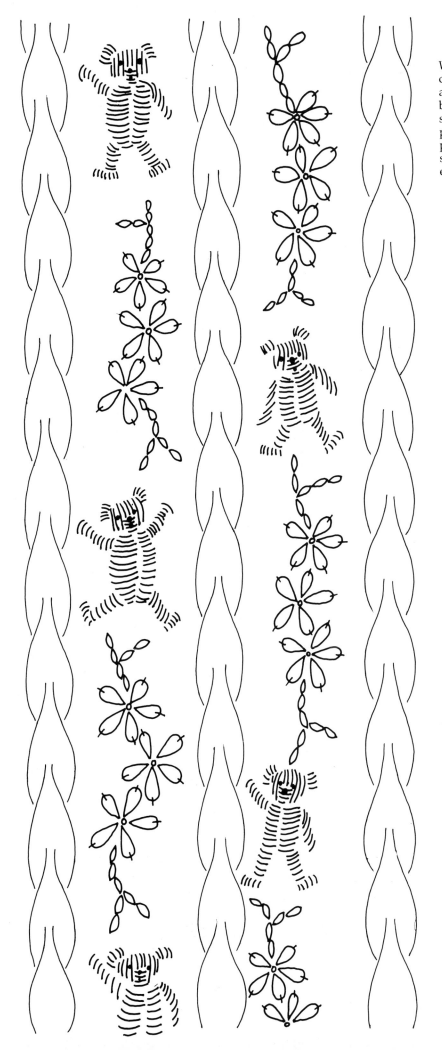

When you have completed the front, back and arms of the cardigan, but before you join the seams, embroider this pattern as described on page 40. The embroidery stitches needed are explained on page 12.

Row 1: k1, p21, k6, p8, k6, p2, k1.
Row 2: k3, p6, k8, p6, k22.
Repeat these 2 rows twice.
Row 7: k1, p21, sl the next 3 sts onto a cable needle and hold at back of work, k3, k3 from cable needle (this will be described in future as C6R), p8, C6R, p2, k1.
Row 8: work as for row 2.
Row 9: k1, p12, k1, (p8, k6) twice, p2, k1.
Row 10: k3, (p6, k8) twice, p1, k13.
Row 11: k1, p11, k2, (p8, k6) twice, p2, k1.
Row 12: k3, (p6, k8) twice, p2, k12.
Row 13: k1, p10, k3, (p8, k6) twice, p2, k1.
Row 14: k3, (p6, k8) twice, p3, k11.
*Row 15: k1, p7, C6R, (p8, C6R) twice, p2, k1.
Row 16: k3, (p6, k8) 3 times.
Row 17: k1, p7, k6, (p8, k6) twice, p2, k1.
Row 18: work as for row 16.
Repeat the last 2 rows twice more.*
The 8 rows from * to * form the pattern and are repeated throughout. Cont in pattern, inc 1 st at beg of the 4th cable row (counting from beg of the work on the cable rib nearest the front edge). Inc 1 st at the same edge on every following cable row until you have 51 sts. Cont in pattern working even until 12 cable rows from the beg have been worked. Work 5 more rows of pattern (ending with a WS row). **NOTE:** All increased sts should be purled – do not introduce another cable rib.
Shape armhole (RS): bind off 6 sts, p7, work in pattern to end. Cont in pattern, dec 1 st at beg of the next 3 alt rows (42 sts). Cont to work even until 16 cable rows from beg have been worked. Work 6 rows in pattern (ending at the neck edge).
Shape neck: bind off 7 sts at beg of the next row and, cont in pattern, dec 1 st at neck edge on the next and every following alt row until you have 32 sts. Cont to work even in pattern until 19 cable rows have been worked from beg. Work back to armhole edge. **Shape shoulder:** bind off 12 sts at beg of the next row and 10 sts at beg of the following 2 alt rows. Fasten off.

Right front
Using No.6 needles and main color, cast on 45 sts.
Row 1: k1, p2, k6, p8, k6, p21, k1.
Row 2: k22, p6, k8, p6, k3.
Repeat these 2 rows twice.
Row 7: k1, p2, slip the next 3 sts onto a cable needle and hold at front of work, k3, k3 from cable needle (this will be described in future

as C6L), p8, C6L, p21, k1.
Row 8: work as for row 2.
Row 9: k1, p2, (k6, p8) twice, k1, p12, k1.
Row 10: k13, p1, (k8, p6) twice, k3.
Row 11: k1, p2, (k6, p8) twice, k2, p11, k1.
Row 12: k12, p2, (k8, p6) twice, k3.
Row 13: k1, p2, (k6, p8) twice, k3 p10, k1.
Row 14: k11, p3, (k8, p6) twice, k3.
*Row 15: k1, p2, C6L, (p8, C6L) twice, p7, k1.
Row 16: (k8, p6) 3 times, k3.
Row 17: k1, p2, k6, (p8, k6) twice, p7, k1.
Row 18: Work as for row 16.
Repeat the last 2 rows twice more.*
The last 8 rows from * to * form the pattern and are repeated throughout. From this point, work to match left front, increasing at the side edge at the end of the cable rows (instead of at the beg) and reading C6L instead of C6R. Reverse all other shapings.

Back
Using No.6 needles and main color, cast on 86 sts.
Row 1: k1, p18, (k6, p8) 3 times, k6, p18, k1.
Row 2: k19, (p6, k8) 3 times, p6, k19.
Repeat these 2 rows twice more.
Row 7: k1, p18, (C6R, p8) twice, C6L, p8, C6L, p18, k1.
Row 8: Work as for row 2.
Row 9: k1, p9, k1, (p8, k6) 4 times, p8, k1, p9, k1.
Row 10: k10, p1, (k8, p6) 4 times, k8, p1, k10.
Row 11: k1, p8, k2, (p8, k6) 4 times, p8, k2, p8, k1.
Row 12: k9, p2, (k8, p6) 4 times, k8, p2, k9.
Row 13: k1, p7, k3, (p8, k6) 4 times, p8, k3, p7, k1.
Row 14: k8, p3, (k8, p6) 4 times, k8, p3, k8.
*Row 15: k1, p4, (C6R, p8) 3 times, (C6L, p8) twice, C6L, p4, k1.
Row 16: k5, (p6, k8) 5 times, p6, k5.
Row 17: k1, p4, (k6, p8) 5 times, k6, p4, k1.
Row 18: Work as for row 16.
Repeat the last 2 rows twice.*
The 8 rows from * to * form the pattern and are repeated throughout.
Cont in pattern, inc 1 st at each end of the 4th cable row (counting cable rows from beg of the work on the center cable) and cont to inc 1 st at each end of every following cable row until you have 98 sts. **NOTE:** All increased sts should be purled – do not start a new cable. Cont to work even in pattern until 12 cable rows from beg have been worked. Work 5 rows in pattern.

Shape armholes: bind off 4 sts at beg of the next 2 rows, then dec 1 st at each end of the next row and every following alt row until 86 sts remain. Cont to work even until 19 cable rows have been worked from the beg. Work pattern for 1 row. **Shape shoulders**: bind off 12 sts at beg of the next 2 rows. Bind off 10 sts at beg of the next 4 rows. Bind off remaining 20 sts.

Sleeves (Make 2)

Using No.6 needles and main color, cast on 48 sts.
Row 1: k1, p13, k6, p8, k6, p13, k1.
Row 2: k14, p6, k8, p6, k14.
Repeat these 2 rows twice.
Row 7: k1, p13, C6R, p8, C6L, p13, k1.
Row 8: work as for row 2.
These 8 rows form the pattern and are repeated throughout. Cont in pattern, inc 1 st at each end of the next and every following 6th row until you have 78 sts (purling all extra sts). Cont to work even in pattern until 15 cable rows have been worked from beg. Work pattern for 1 row. **Shape cap**: next row (RS): bind off 8 sts at beg of next 2 rows, then dec 1 st at each end of next and every following alt row until 48 sts remain. Cont to work even until 20 cable rows have been worked from the beg. Work pattern for 1 more row. Cont as follows:
Row 1: k2 tog, p10, p2 tog, k6, p2 tog, p4, p2 tog, k6, p2 tog, p10, k2 tog.
Row 2: k2 tog, k10, p6, k6, p6, k10, k2 tog.
Row 3: k2 tog, p7, p2 tog, k6, p2 tog, p2, p2 tog, k6, p2 tog, p7, k2 tog.
Row 4: k2 tog, k7, p6, k4, p6, k7, k2 tog.

Row 5: k2 tog, p4, p2 tog, k6, (p2 tog) twice, k6, p2 tog, p4, k2 tog.
Row 6: k2 tog, k4, p6, k2, p6, k4, k2 tog.
Row 7: k2 tog, p1, p2 tog, C6R, p2 tog, C6L, p2 tog, p1, k2 tog.
Row 8: k2 tog, k1, p6, k1, p6, k1, k2 tog.
Bind off.

Embroidery

Press all pieces lightly on the wrong side. Following the embroidery chart, work the teddies in yellow using satin stitch. Work the daisies in daisy stitch using red and blue and making yellow French knots in the center. Using green wool, work the flower stems in green chain stitch (all the embroidery stitches are described in Techniques, *see* page 12). The teddies' eyes and noses are worked using a small single stitch in black wool.

Finishing

Using flat seams throughout, join side and sleeve seams and set in the sleeves.

Crochet edge and buttonholes

With RS of work facing and using a medium-sized crochet hook, start at the bottom right front and with blue wool make a single chain of crochet up the right front, around the neck and down the left front. Evenly space eight pins up the left front to mark positions for buttons. Using red wool, make a second chain of crochet up the right front working 4 chain sts instead of a single stitch opposite the button markers. Press lightly.
Stitch on the buttons.

SPENCER BEAR AND SON

A pair of cuddly bears that are worked in a choice of yarns using fur stitch. Papa bear is 21¼in tall when seated, while his son stands approximately 13¼in tall.

Stitches (Fur stitch)

Row 1 (RS): k1, *k1, but do not drop stitch off left-hand needle, bring yarn forward between needles and wind over left thumb to form a loop. Take yarn between needles to back and k the same stitch again, dropping it off the left-hand needle. Bring yarn forward between needles and take it over right-hand needle to make a loop, pass the 2 sts just worked over this loop and off right-hand needle. K next st,* rep from * to *.
Row 2: knit.
Row 3: k2, rep from * to *.
Row 4: knit.

Body

Using No.6 needles, cast on 22/44 sts. K 1/2 rows. Next row: k, inc into every st (44/88 sts). Repeat these 2 rows once more (88/176

Materials

Wendy Dolce brown (100) or Merino DK camel (236) – **large bear** 1000gm; **small bear** 300gm. One pair of amber glass eyes. Polyester stuffing. Small amount of black wool.

Needles

One pair of No.6 needles.

Gauge

Using No.6 needles and measured over st st, 24 sts and 32 rows = 4in square.

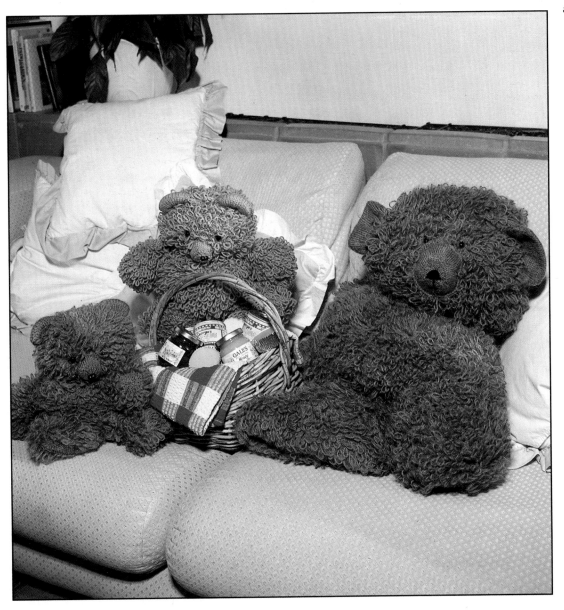

sts). Begin working in fur st, starting at row 1 * for 27/54 rows. Next row: (k2 tog, k18, k2 tog) 4/8 times (80/160 sts). K 1/2 rows. Next row: (k2 tog, k16, k2 tog) 4/8 times (72/144 sts). Still working in fur st, work 15/30 rows even. Next row: **k2 tog, rep from ** to end (36/72 sts). K 2/4 rows. Next row: k2 tog across row (18/36 sts). Work 2/4 rows. Bind off.

Head

Work as for body to *. Work in fur st for 21/42 rows, then work as for body until you have 72/144 sts. Work 11/22 rows. Cont by shaping as for body until you have 18/36 sts. Bind off.

Legs (Make 2)

Starting at the foot, cast on 44/88 sts. K 1/2 rows. Next row: k17/34, (inc into next st)

When you come to make up the teddy bear, sew the seams in the order given on page 43.

42

10/20 times. K17/34 (54/108 sts). K 1/2 rows. Next row: k22/44, (inc into next st) 10/20 times, k22/44 (64/128 sts). Begin working in fur st from row 1 and work 7/14 rows. Cont working in fur st. Next row: k22/44, (k2 tog) 10/20 times, k22/44, (54/108 sts). K 1/2 rows. Next row: k17, (k2 tog) 10/20 times, k17 (44/88 sts). Work 17/34 rows even in fur st. Bind off loosely.

Arms (Make 2)

Starting at shoulder, cast on 8/16 sts. K 1/2 rows. Begin working in fur st from row 1, inc 1 st at each end of every row until you have 44/88 sts. Work in fur st for 16/32 rows even. Next row: k2 tog, right across row 22/44 sts. K 1/2 rows. Repeat the last 2 rows once (11/22 sts). Next row: k1, (k2 tog) 5/10 times (6/12 sts). Break off yarn, thread it through the remaining sts. Draw up tight and fasten off.

Nose

Cast on 32/64 sts. Work 4/8 rows in st st.
Next row: (k2 tog, k6) 4/8 times (28/56 sts).
Next row: (k5, k2 tog) 4/8 times (24/48 sts).
Next row: (k2 tog, k4) 4/8 times (20/40 sts).
Next row: (k3, k2 tog) 4/8 times (16/32 sts).
Next row: (k2 tog, k2) 4/8 times (12/24 sts).
Next row: (k1, k2 tog) 4/8 times (8/16 sts).

Break off yarn and thread it back through the remaining sts. Draw up tight and fasten off.

Ears (Make 2)

Cast on 18/32 sts and work in st st for 6/12 rows. Dec 1 st at each end of the next 2/4 rows. Work 1/2 rows, inc 1 st at each end of the next 2/4 rows. Work in st st for 6/12 rows. Bind off.

Finishing

Sew all seams invisibly working on the wrong side. Fold head in half and join center back seam. Stuff firmly. Fold nose in half and join seam. Sew to head, stuffing as you go. With black wool, embroider nose over center seam. Attach eyes to head either side of top of nose. Join head seam. Join and stuff body. Stitch head firmly to body with an overcast stitch. Fold ears in half and stitch short ends together. Stuff lightly and sew along bottom seam and gather slightly, sew to head. Fold arms in half and sew up sleeves leaving a 2in opening at the narrow end. Stuff and stitch to body. Fold legs in half and join seam which is at the center back, stuff and stitch firmly to body in sitting position.

TEDDY BOOTIES

Materials
Wendy Peter Pan DK yarn – spring-lamb (868) and lemon (803): less than 50gm of each. ¾yd of ⅜in wide satin ribbon. Scrap of brown wool for embroidery.

Needles
One set of 4 double-pointed No.5 needles.

Gauge
Using No.5 needles and measured over st st, 24 sts and 30 rows = 4in square.

A pretty pair of teddy booties to keep baby's toes snug.

Booties
Using No.5 double-pointed needles and

white, cast on 10 sts. Work in garter stitch for 38 rows. Join yellow, p 1 row. Next row: k twice into every stitch (20 sts). Next row: p12, turn, k4, turn, p3, turn, k2, turn, p3, turn, k4, turn, p5, turn, k2 tog, k1, k2 tog, k to end. Work 3 rows in st st. Next row: *k4, k2 tog, rep from * to end. Next row: *p3, p2 tog, rep from * across row. Next row: *k2, k2 tog, rep from * across row. Next row: k2 tog across row, then p2 tog across row to last st, p1. Next row: k2 tog, k1, k2 tog. Next row: sl 1, p2 tog, psso, fasten off.

Change to white and, starting halfway across cast-on edge with RS facing, pick up and knit 5 sts across heel, 18 sts across side edge, 10 sts across last row of white (under teddy's head), 18 sts down second edge, 5 sts across heel. Work 5 rounds in st st. **Shape toe:** k31, ssk, turn (leaving remaining 23 sts unworked). Next row: k7, k2 tog, turn, k7, ssk, turn. Next row: k7, ssk, turn. Repeat the last 2 rows 6 times more, turn, work to end. Next row: *k1, yo, k2 tog, rep from * to end. K 1 round. Bind off knitwise.

Finishing

Embroider a knot in brown on the end of teddy's snout, with a small vertical and horizontal line beneath for his nose. Make two knots for eyes. Turn teddy's head back onto bootie toe and join by stitching around face (leaving ears free). Thread a length of satin ribbon through eyelets at top of bootie and tie in a bow.

BEARS AND BEES SWEATER

Materials
Wendy Aran Tweed –
crofter (590): 550gm.
Wendy Soft Touch – sable
(62): 50gm. Wendy Aran
– antelope (516): 50gm.
Wendy Action Knit – blue
(513): 100gm; black (530):
50gm. Wendy Family
Choice DK (used double)
– yellow (267): 50gm.

Needles
One pair of No.6 and one
pair of No.8 needles; one
No.6, 24in circular needle.

Gauge
Using No.6 needles and
measured over st st, 18 sts
and 22 rows = 4in square.
Ribs worked on No.6
needles.

This boxy, tweedy aran-weight sweater is
worked using both the intarsia and fairisle
methods (*see* pages 7–8).

Front
Using No.6 needles and main color, cast on
96 sts. Work in k1, p1 rib for 2¼in.

Follow the chart opposite
to complete the front and
back of the sweater. The
dotted line around the
honey-pot chart indicates
the area of the pocket that
should be knitted into the
front. The bear chart
should be incorporated
into the right sleeve and
the two bee charts into
the left sleeve as
described on page 49.

Chart 1

Chart 2

Change to No.8 needles and begin following chart in st st for 18 rows. **Pocket opening**: next row: k46, slip the last 34 sts from the right-hand needle onto a stitch holder, k to end. Next row: p50, turn, cast on 34 sts, turn, p to end. Cont following chart working new sts in main color only. Work even to neck shaping. Next row (RS): k45, bind off 6, k45. Working on the last set of sts only, *p back to neck edge, turn, bind off 5 sts, k to end, rep from * once more. P back to neck edge, turn, bind off 4 sts, k to end. Bind off 3 sts at neck edge on the next alt row and 2 sts at neck edge on the following alt row. Work 1 row. Bind off loosely. Rejoin yarn at neck edge on remaining sts and shape to match first side. **Pocket:** pick up the 34 sts held for pocket and work the honey-pot chart until it is complete. Work 1 row. Change to No.6 needles, k1, p1 rib for 3 rows. Bind off. Stitch pocket into position.

Back

Work as for front but do not work pocket, simply knit honey-pot motif into main body of sweater in position as shown. Cont following the chart to back neck shaping. Next row (RS): k70 sts, slip the last 44 sts worked off the right-hand needle onto a stitch holder, k to end. Turn, p26, turn. Bind off loosely. Rejoin yarn to other side of neck at inner edge. Work 1 row. Bind off loosely.

Right sleeve

Using No.6 needles and main color, cast on 50 sts. Work in k1, p1 rib for 2¼in. Change to No.8 needles* and work 3 rows in st st, inc 1 st at each end of the next row. Work 2 rows in st st. Begin working from

bear chart setting up pattern as follows: k15, k across the 22 sts of the chart, k15. Complete the chart, inc 1 st at each end of the next row and every following 4th row until you have 100 sts. Work 3 rows. Bind off.

Left sleeve

Work as for right sleeve to *. Cont in st st, inc 1 st at each end of every 4th row until you have 100 sts. *At the same time*, when you have just completed your increase to 82 sts, work first bee chart, setting up pattern as follows: k42, k the 14 sts of chart, k26. Working shaping as before, complete this chart and cont until you have just worked your increase to 92 sts. Next row (RS): k27, k the 14 sts of the second bee chart, k51. Cont shaping as before and complete chart in pattern as established. When you have completed your shaping to 100 sts, work 3 rows. Bind off.

Neckband

Sew both shoulder seams together and, using a No.6 circular needle, pick up and k 168 sts evenly around the neck. Work in k1, p1 rib for 1½in. Bind off loosely in ribbing. Slip st bound-off edge to pick-up edge. **Collar:** using No.6 needles and main color, cast on 124 sts. Work in k1, p1 rib for 5¼in. Bind off. Sew bound-off edge of collar to inside seam of neckband, leaving a center front opening.

Finishing

Join sleeves to sweater using a narrow backstitch. Join side and sleeve seams using flat seams.

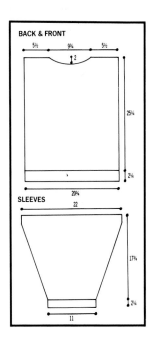

LITTLE BEARS

Materials
For two white and two brown teddies: Wendy Soft Touch – white (54) and sable (62): 50gm. Wendy Family Choice Chunky – small amounts in assorted colors. Scraps of black DK wool for eyes and noses and a small quantity of polyester stuffing. **Baby carriage toy** 1¼yd of elastic cord; 11 wooden beads. **Mobile** ¾ × 14¼in and 1½ × 5½in lengths of stiff wire and some nylon thread.

Needles
One pair of No.6 needles.

Gauge
Using No.6 needles and measured over st st, 20 sts and 20 rows = 4in square to produce a teddy 5in tall.

These little mohair bears are quick to knit and make ideal gifts at Christmas time. String them together and you have a delightful baby carriage toy, or make your own nursery mobile.

TEDDY

(Half body)

Beginning at legs, cast on 10 sts in mohair and work 18 rows in st st. **Shape arms**: k4, bind off 1 st, slip last stitch back onto left-hand needle, cast on 18 sts and k to end. Work 4 rows in st st. Next row: p5, bind off 18 sts. P4, break yarn, slide stitches to end of needle. Work another half body in the same way but do not break yarn.

Head

RS: k across the remaining 18 sts, p 1 row. Next row: k10, turn, p4, turn, k3, turn, p2, turn, k3, turn, p4, turn, k2 tog twice, k to end. Work 3 rows in st st. Next row: *k4, k2 tog, rep once from *, k4. Next row: p. Next row: *k3, k2 tog, rep once from *, k4. Next row: p. Next row: *k2, k2 tog, rep from * to last 2 sts, k2. Break yarn and thread it back through loops, pull up tightly and secure.

Finishing

Sew up center back, front and arm seams of body, leaving a small hole in back for stuffing. Stuff body and head. Using a small piece of black wool, make a knot for teddy's nose on the end of his snout. Make a small vertical and horizontal stitch below the nose for his mouth. Make two knots for the eyes.

Ears

Pick up 3 sts from the side of teddy's head,

inc once into each st (6 sts). Work 2 rows.
Bind off. Repeat for other side. Stitch sides of
ears to head.

SWEATER

Using No.6 needles and bright chunky wool,
cast on 11 sts. Work 1 row in k1, p1 rib. K 12
rows. Cast on 7 sts at beg of the next 2 rows.
K 8 rows. Next row: k8, bind off 9, k8. Next
row: k8, cast on 9, k8. K 7 rows. Bind off 7
sts at beg of the next 2 rows, k 12 rows.
Work 1 row in k1, p1 rib. Bind off.

Finishing
Place sweater over teddy's head, sew up
underarm and side seams.

BABY CARRIAGE TOY

Using a blunt needle, thread the elastic
through 4 beads, one bear, one bead, one
bear, one bead, one bear, one bead, one
bear, four beads. Form a loop of elastic at
each end and knot, threading the waste
elastic back through the end beads.

MOBILE

Take the two longer lengths of wire and
make small loops at each end. Cross the two
wires in the middle and close firmly with a
pair of pliers. Hang four lengths of nylon
thread off the loops and attach the shorter
lengths of wire (with loops at each end). Tie
lengths of nylon to the center head of eight
teddies and hang them at each end of the
shorter lengths of wire.

THE BEAR'N-STEINS

A contemporary pair of bears with a love for traditional knitwear.

MR & MRS BEAR'N-STEIN

Right leg
Using No.5 needles, cast on 32 sts. Work in st st for 8 rows.*
Next row: k9, k2 tog, k7, k2 tog, k12.
Next row: p12, p2 tog, p5, p2 tog, p9.
Next row: k9, k2 tog, k3, k2 tog, k12.
Next row: p12, p2 tog, p1, p2 tog, p9 (23 sts).

Work 26 rows in st st, leave sts on a spare needle.

Left leg
Work as for right leg to *.
Next row: k12, k2 tog, k7, k2 tog, k9.
Next row: p9, p2 tog, p5, p2 tog, p12.
Next row: k12, k2 tog, k3, k2 tog, k9.
Next row: p9, p2 tog, p1, p2 tog, p12.
Work 26 rows in st st. K across sts for both legs on next row (46 sts). Work 36 rows in st st for body. **Shape shoulders:** next row: k8. Bind off 10 sts. K10, bind off 10 sts. K8.

Materials
Wendy Ascot DK wool – **male teddy** thatch (403): 150gm; **female teddy** hazelnut (411): 150gm. **Fairisle sweater** ecru (1) (A) – plum (408) (B), hazelnut (411) and black (423): 50gm of each. **Female's guernsey** Wendy Family Choice Aran – cream (524): 50gm. **Skirt** Ascot DK wool – red (426): 50gm. **Male's trousers** Ascot DK wool – lovat (437): 50gm. Small button. Small bag polyester stuffing.

Needles
One pair of No.5 and one pair of No.6 needles. One set of double-pointed No.4 needles. One cable needle.

Gauge
Using No.5 needles and measured over st st, 24 sts and 32 rows = 4in square. This gauge produces a bear approximately 13¾in tall.

Follow this chart when you make the fairisle sweater.

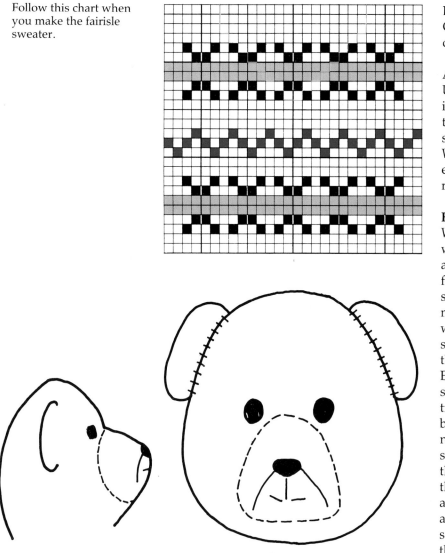

The dotted line around the muzzle indicates the line of the gathering thread.

Head

Ignoring the bound-off shoulders, p twice into every stitch (52 sts) – i.e., the shoulders will form 2 loops which will eventually be seamed at the top. Work in st st for 4 rows.
Shape muzzle: k20, k2 tog, k8, sl 1, k1, psso, k20.
Next row and every alt row: purl.
Row 3: k20, k2 tog, k6, sl 1, k1, psso, k20.
Row 5: k20, k2 tog, k4, sl 1, k1, psso, k20.
Row 7: k20, k2 tog, k2, sl 1, k1, psso, k20 (44 sts).
Work 6 rows in st st.
Next row (WS): p18, p2 tog 13 times (31 sts).
Work 9 rows in st st.
Next row: k2 tog 15 times, k1 (16 sts).
Next row: p2 tog 8 times (8 sts). Slip sts off needle and break yarn. Thread yarn back through sts and gather up tightly.

Ears (Make 2)

Cast on 14 sts, work 10 rows in st st, then cast off.

Arms

Using No.5 needles, cast on 16 sts. Working in st st, inc 1 st at each end of every row 3 times (22 sts). Work 4 rows even, then dec 1 st at each end of every row 3 times (16 sts). Work 13 rows even. **Shape top:** dec 1 st at each end of every row 4 times. Bind off remaining 8 sts. Repeat for second arm.

Finishing

Working all seams on the wrong side of your work, fold legs and feet in half lengthwise and sew up inside leg seams. Stuff legs and feet firmly. Join back and back head seam, stuffing as you go. Add extra stuffing to muzzle, making sure that it protrudes. Then, working with length of main color yarn and starting at the neck, thread the yarn around the muzzle and gather it up (*see* diagram). Embroider eyes by working an overcast stitch in black, in position as shown. Sew a triangle for the nose and overcast stitch in black. Embroider mouth and stitch from nose down to mouth using three large stitches (*see* diagram). Fold ears in half, with the longest edges together, and stitch along the bottom, gather slightly along this edge and sew into position as indicated. Sew up arm seams to where top shaping begins and stuff. Stitch arm-tops neatly onto body so that the center arm-top touches the center shoulder. Stitch across shoulders.

FAIRISLE SWEATER

Front

Using No.5 needles and main color, cast on 28 sts.
Row 1: k1A, *p2B, k2A, rep from * to last st, k1A.
Row 2: p1A, *k2B, p2B, rep from * to last st, p1A.
Repeat these last 2 rows once more, then begin following chart in st st to neck shaping.
Next row (RS): work pattern for 13 sts, turn, dec 1 st, p to end. Working on this side of the neck only, dec 1 st at neck edge on the next 6 rows (6 sts). Work 3 rows. Bind off. Rejoin yarn at neck edge, bind off 2 sts, work to end. Bind off 1 st at neck edge on next 7 rows. Work 2 rows. Bind off.

Back

Work as for front ignoring neck shaping. Work to shoulder line. Bind off.

Sleeves (Make 2)

Work as for front until the row of zig-zags has been completed. Work 3 rows in main color only. Bind off.

Neckband

Join shoulder seams. With a set of 4 double-ended No.4 needles and with RS of work facing, start at the bottom of the V-neck and pick up 48 sts evenly around neck. Work back and forth in k1, p1 rib and main color only for 3 rows. Bind off in plum.

PANTS

Using No.5 needles and a contrasting color, cast on 30 sts.
Row 1 (RS): *p2, k1, rep from * to end.
Row 2: *p1, k2, rep from * to end. Repeat these 2 rows until work measures 5½in. Work 5 rows in st st. Bind off. Make the second leg in the same way.

Finishing

Sew in all ends on the fairisle sweater. Sew sleeves to body. Join side and sleeve seams. Lay trouser legs side by side. Fold each leg in half lengthwise. Join legs together at center front and back from the st st waistband downwards for 1½in to form the crotch. Join inside leg seams. Sew small button center front on trouser waistband. Fold up lower edges of pants to form cuffs.

ARAN SWEATER

Front

Using No.6 needles and ecru aran-weight wool, cast on 34 sts. Work 4 rows in k1, p1 rib. Cont in pattern as follows:
Row 1: k4, slip next 3 sts onto a cable needle and hold at front of work. K3, k3 from cable needle, k6, p2, k6, slip 3 sts onto a cable needle and hold at back of work. K3, k3 from cable needle, k4.
Row 2: p15, k4, p15.
Row 3: k14, p6, k14.
Row 4: k13, p8, k13.
Row 5: k4, slip next 3 sts onto a cable needle, hold at front of work, k3, k3 from cable needle, k2, p10, k2, slip next 3 sts onto a cable needle and hold at back of work, k3, k3 from cable needle, k4.
Row 6: p12, k10, p12.
Row 7: k13, p8, k13.
Row 8: p14, k6, p14.
Row 9: k4, slip next 3 sts onto a cable needle and hold at front of work, k3, k3 from cable needle, k5, p4, k5, slip next 3 sts onto a cable needle and hold at back, k3, k3 from cable needle, k4.
Row 10: p16, k1, k4 from next stitch, pass first 3 sts over 4th stitch to make bobble, p16. These 10 rows make your pattern. Repeat them twice more. K 1 row. Next row: p8, k18, p8. Next row: bind off 8 sts. K18, k8. Next row, bind off 8 sts. K18, turn, bind off remaining 18 sts.

Back

Work exactly as for front.

Sleeves (Make 2)

Using No.6 needles, cast on 34 sts. K1, p1 rib for 4 rows, then work in knit only until sleeve measures 3¼in. Bind off.

Finishing

Join shoulder seams. Join sleeves to sweater, join side and sleeve seams.

SKIRT

Using No.6 needles and DK wool, cast on 66 sts. K 2 rows, then work in st st, starting with a knit row until skirt measures 5¼in, ending with a p row. Next row: *k1, k2 tog, rep from * to end, k1. Work 4 rows in k1, p1 rib. Bind off. Join side seam.

RUPERT BEAR SWEATER

Materials
Wendy Ascot DK wool –
blue (425): 550gm; yellow
(6): 100gm; black (423):
100gm; white (400): 50gm;
red (426): 50gm. 3 buttons
¾in in diameter.

Needles
One pair of No.4 and one
pair of No.6 needles. One
cable needle.

Gauge
Using No.6 needles and
worked over st st, 24 sts
and 32 rows = 4in square.
Ribs worked on No.4
needles.

Rupert Bear has been a firm family favorite
for generations. Our designer sweater,
worked in cable and moss stitch diamonds,
is strictly for the more experienced knitter.

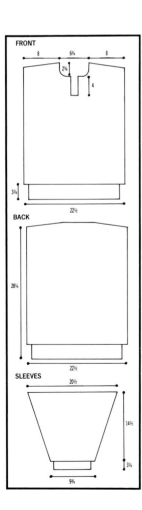

Back

Using No.4 needles, cast on 111 sts and work in k1, p1 rib (row 1: k1, *p1, k1, rep from * to end. Row 2: p1, *k1, p1, rep from * to end). Repeat these 2 rows until work measures 3¼in, inc 27 sts evenly across last row (138 sts).

Change to No.6 needles and work from chart with cables at sides setting up pattern as follows:

Row 1: sl 1, p2, k8, p2, k8, p2, work chart over 92 sts, p2, k8, p2, k8, p2, k1 tbl.

Row 2: sl 1, k2, p8, k2, p8, k2, work chart over 92 sts, k2, p8, k2, p8, k2, k1 tbl.

Working sts in pattern as established, cont to work cables on 9th and then every following 8th row on side panels as follows:

Row 9: sl 1, k2, C8F, p2, C8F, p2, work chart over 92 sts, p2, C8B, p2, C8B, p2, k1 tbl.

Work rows 1–130 of chart, then repeat rows 2–68 (total of 197 rows).

Shape shoulders: next row (RS): bind off 12 sts at beg of the next 6 rows, then bind off 13 sts at beg of the next 2 rows, leave remaining sts on a holder for collar.

Front

Work as for back until row 130 of chart has been completed. Now repeat from row 2 again, but this time working center diamond (Rupert motif) all in moss stitch. Cont until row 14 has been completed.

Front opening: work 65 sts from chart and turn, work on these sts for first side, cont from chart for a further 31 rows.

Neck shaping: next row (WS): bind off 4 sts, work to end, dec 1 st at neck edge on next 12 rows, then cont until work measures same as back to shoulder.

Shape shoulder: next row (RS): bind off 12 sts at beg of the next and 2 following alt rows, work 1 row, bind off remaining sts. Rejoin yarn to remaining sts, bind off 8 sts at center front, work on remaining sts to match first side, reversing shaping.

Sleeves (Make 2)

Using No.4 needles, cast on 50 sts and work in k1, p1 rib for 3¼in, inc 10 sts evenly across last row (60 sts).

Change to No.6 needles and work from chart, starting at Row 5, and inc 1 st at each end of every third row as indicated, when there are 92 sts on needle. Cont from chart, inc at each end of every 3rd row as before until you have 126 sts. Cont working inc sts in moss stitch as established. After last inc, cont until row 120 has been completed. Bind off all sts.

Buttonband

Join shoulder seams. Using No.4 needles and with RS of work facing, pick up and knit approximately 24 sts down left front neck opening. Work in k1, p1 rib until band fits neatly across center front (8 sts). Bind off in ribbing.

Mark position for 3 buttons on center row of band, the first on 3rd st from center front, the last on 3rd st from neck edge and the other spaced evenly between.

Buttonhole band

Work as for buttonband, working buttonholes opposite marked positions as follows.

Buttonhole row

At each marked position, k2 tog, yrn.

Collar

Using No.4 needles and with RS of work facing, starting just off center (towards neck) of buttonhole band, pick up and knit 3 sts from band, 4 bound-off neck sts, approximately 20 sts up right front neck, back neck 40 sts, approximately 20 sts down left front neck, 4 bound-off neck sts and 3 sts from buttonband. Work in k1, p1 rib for 3¼in. Bind off loosely in ribbing.

Finishing

Set sleeves in place, the center of sleeve to shoulder seam and set the rest evenly at each side. Sew into place. Sew button and buttonhole band at center front bound-off sts, with the buttonband underneath. Sew side and sleeve seams. Sew on buttons to match buttonholes. Embroider scarf as indicated on photograph, using backstitch.

The chart overleaf (on pages 58-9) should be followed to complete the front and the back of the sweater and also the sleeves. The key for the chart is given below, and for instructions on making a bobble (see page 9). The black lines on Rupert's scarf should be embroidered, using backstitch, when the sweater is complete.

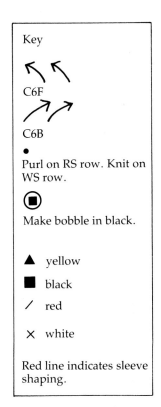

Key

C6F

C6B

• Purl on RS row. Knit on WS row.

⬤ Make bobble in black.

▲ yellow

■ black

/ red

✕ white

Red line indicates sleeve shaping.

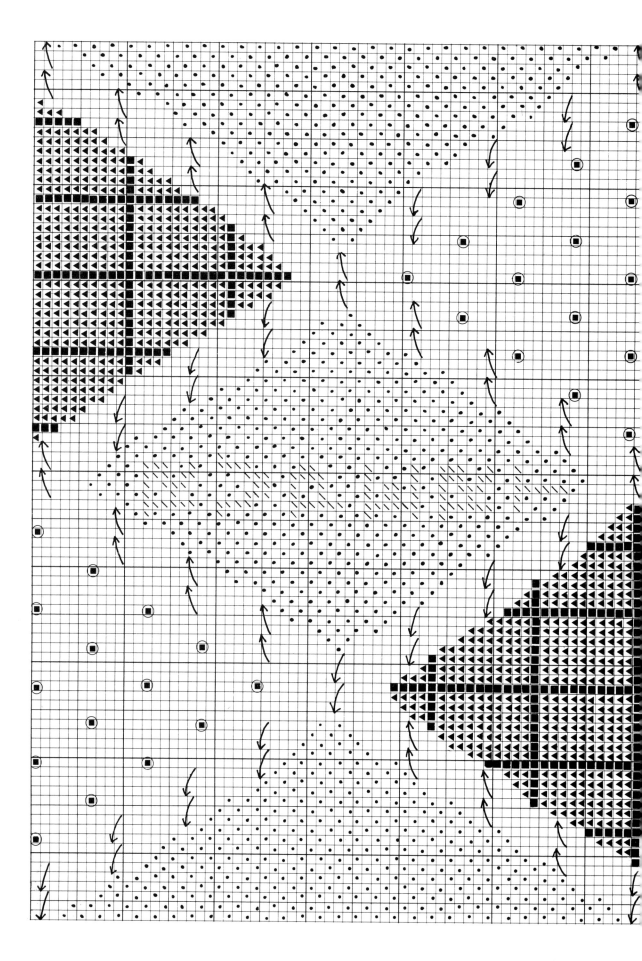

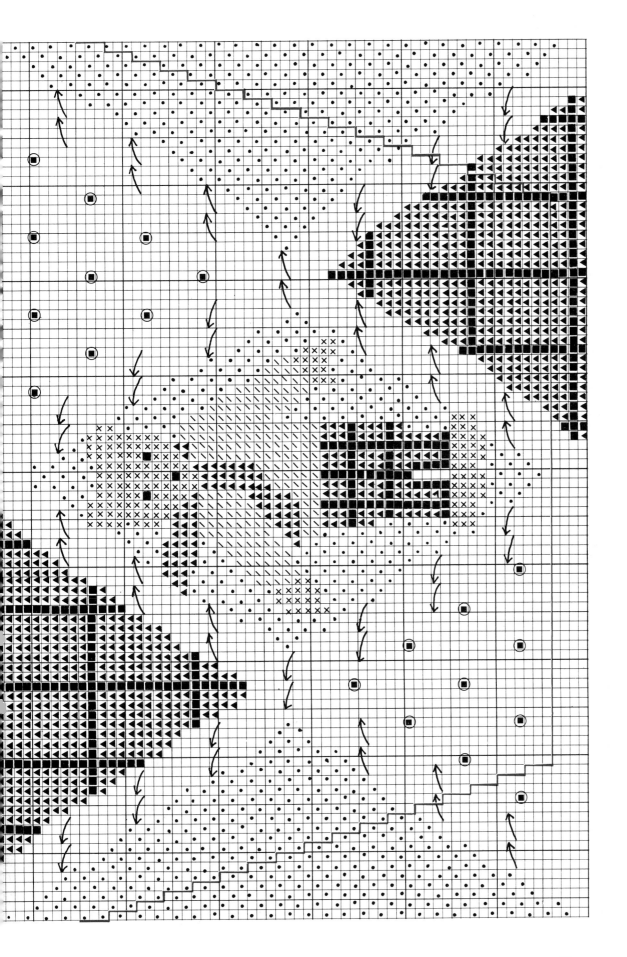

SNOWBALL SLEEPING-BAG

Snug as a teddy in a rug, this woolly sleeping-bag for a baby aged 3 months to one year, is worked in a cable check with motifs using the intarsia method (*see* Techniques, page 8).

Materials
Wendy Family Choice DK yarn – red (242): 250gm; colors to match the chart, purity (212), Côte d'Azur (216), Sahara (202), black (247), amber fire (267), neon flash (903) and emerald isle (205): less than 50gm of each. A 12in long nylon separating zipper.

Needles
One pair of No.4 and one pair of No.6 needles; one cable needle.

Gauge
Using No.6 needles and measured over st st, 22 sts and 32 rows = 4in square.

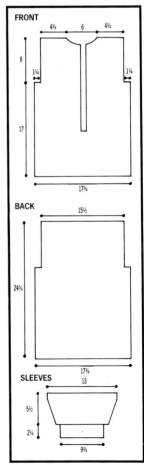

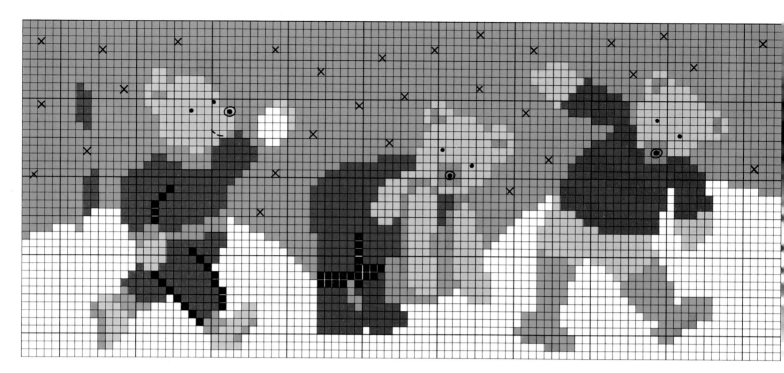

Incorporate the top chart into both the front and the back of the sleeping-bag. The crosses indicate where bobbles should be made in white (*see* page 9), and the dots indicate where the bears' noses should be completed, in black, by knitting three from one stitch and passing the first two stitches over the fourth loop.

The lower chart should be followed to complete the sleeves (*see* page 64). The crosses indicate where bobbles should be worked in white (*see* page 9).

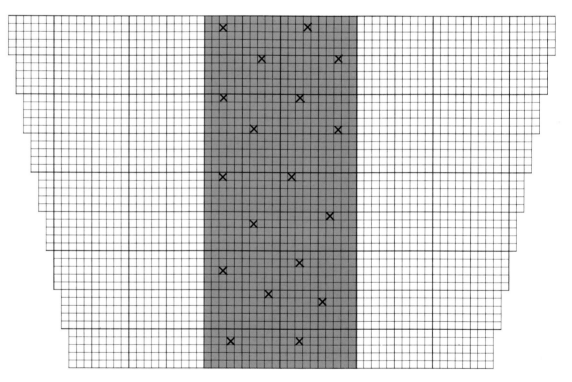

Pattern: Cable check

Rows 1, 3, 5 and 7: k12, p12.

Row 2 and alt rows: k the p sts and p the k sts of the previous row.

Row 9: cross 2R (slip 2 sts onto a cable needle and hold at back of work, k next 2 sts, then k the 2 sts from cable needle), k4, cross 2L (slip 2 sts onto a cable needle and hold at front of work, k next 2 sts, then k the 2 sts from cable needle), p12.

Rows 11, 13, 15 and 17: work as row 1.

Rows 19, 21, 23 and 25: p12, k12.

Row 27: p12, cross 2R, k4, cross 2L.

Rows 29, 31, 33 and 35: work as row 19.

Row 37: repeat from row 1.

Front

Using No.6 needles and main color, cast on 100 sts. Begin working in pattern, setting it up as follows:

Row 1: k2, repeat row 1 of pattern 4 times across the row, k2.

Row 2: p2, repeat row 2 of pattern 4 times across the row, p2.

Cont in pattern and work the 2 edge sts at either end of the row in st st until 36 rows have been worked.

Next row (RS): working in st st only (and making bobbles for noses and snowflakes as indicated on the chart), begin following chart until it is complete (take care to use separate balls or bobbins of yarn for each color – i.e., do not use the fairisle technique). When the chart is complete, change back to main color and p 1 row.

Zipper opening: begin working in pattern from row 1: starting with k2, repeat pattern twice. Leave remaining 50 sts on a spare needle and cont working in pattern on this first set of 50 sts only. When 56 rows have been worked, **shape armholes:** next row (RS): bind off 7 sts at beg of this row and cont working in pattern for another 40 rows. Next row (WS): **shape neck:** bind off 7 sts at beg of the next row, dec 2 sts at neck edge on the next 2 alt rows and 1 st at neck edge on the next 6 alt rows. Work 6 rows, then bind off. Rejoin yarn at neck edge to sts held for other side and work to match, reversing shaping.

Back

Work as for front until the chart is complete. Cont even in pattern until back matches front to armhole shaping, then bind off 7 sts at beg of next 2 rows. Work even until back matches front to shoulder. Bind off.

Sleeves (Make 2)

Using No.4 needles and main color, cast on 42 sts. Work in k1, p1 rib for 2¼in, inc 14 sts evenly across last row of rib (56 sts). Begin following chart working main color in moss st – i.e., row 1: k1, p1. On row 2 p the k sts and k the p sts of the previous row as they are facing you. Work the blue center panel in st st making bobbles where indicated on the chart. *At the same time*, inc 1 st at each end of every 5th row until you have 72 sts. Work 5 rows even. Bind off.

Finishing

Join one shoulder. Using No.4 needles and main color, pick up and k 75 sts evenly around the neck, beginning at the RS neck edge. K1, p1 rib for 5 rows, bind off. Join sleeves to body, join side and sleeve seams using flat seams throughout. Carefully stitch zipper into place.

TEDDY LEGWARMERS, MITTENS AND HAT

A bright collection of hat, mittens and legwarmers in a teddy and jacquard pattern worked using the fairisle method (*see* Techniques page 7).

Materials
Wendy Family Choice DK wool – green (271): 200gm; ecru (230), yellow (267), rose (269) and black (247): less than 50gm of each.

Needles
One pair of No.4 and one pair of No.6 needles. One pair of No.4 and one pair of No.6 double-pointed needles.

Gauge
Using No.6 needles and measured over st st, 24 sts and 32 rows = 4in square.

Incorporate the charts into the legwarmers, mittens and hat as described. Work one teddy bear only for the mittens.

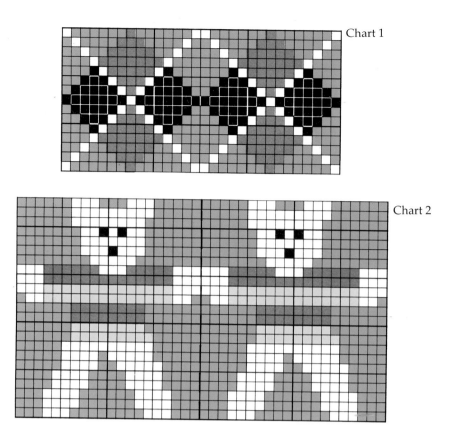

Chart 1

Chart 2

LEGWARMERS

Legs (Make 2)

Using No.4 needles and green (main color), cast on 60 sts. Work in k2, p2 rib for 30 rows, inc 1 st at each end of the last row.

Change to No.6 needles and work 2 rows in st st. *Begin following chart 2, working as follows: k1 in main, work 3 repeats from chart, k1 in main color. Cont in pattern as established until chart is complete. Work 3 rows in main color only, then work chart 1 as follows: work 1 st in main color, work 4 repeats from chart across row, k1 in main color. Work 3 rows in main color only,* repeat from * to *.

Change to No.4 needles, and, dec 1 st at each end of the first row, work 14 rows in double rib. Bind off loosely. Join side seams.

MITTENS

Using No.6 needles and main color, cast on 36 sts. Work 4 rows in st st. Begin working from chart 1, placing pattern as follows: k3, k first row of chart, k3. Cont working of chart until it is complete. Work 3 rows from chart in pattern as established in main color only.

Change to No.4 needles and work 23 rows in k1, p1 rib, inc 7 sts evenly across last row of rib.

Next row (WS): change to No.6 needles and, beginning with a knit row, work in st st for 22 rows. **Divide for thumb:** next row: k 3 sts, place the next 6 sts on a safety-pin, cast on 6 sts, k to end. Work 2 rows in main color only. Begin working from chart 2 until it is complete. Cont in main color only until mitten measures 6in from last row of rib, ending with a WS row. **Shape top:** next row: k1, sl 1, k1, psso, k to last 3 sts, k2 tog, k1. Next row: p 1 row. Repeat these 2 rows until 33 sts remain. Bind off.

Complete thumb: using No.6 double-pointed needles and with RS of work facing, k across 6 sts on safety-pin, pick up and knit 1 st, then pick up and knit 6 sts across cast-on sts of palm (13 sts). Cont in rounds of st st for 2in. **Shape top:** next row: k2 tog to last st, k1 (7 sts). Cut yarn, thread through remaining sts, pull up and fasten off.

Make second mitten to match, reversing shaping.

Finishing

Sew up side seam. Fold cuff back to right side.

TEDDY HAT

Using No.4 double-pointed needles and main color, cast on 134 sts. Work in k1, p1 rib for 1½in, inc 16 sts evenly across last row of rib (150 sts). Change to No.6 double-pointed needles and work 2 rounds in main color only. Begin following chart 1 and work until complete. Work 3 rounds in main color only, then work from chart 2 as follows.

Work 7 teddies across row, then work 13 sts in main color only and complete chart in pattern as established. Work 3 rounds in main color only, repeat chart 1. Cont to work even in main color only until hat measures 9in. Next row: k2 tog, repeat across row. Break yarn and thread it back through the remaining 75 sts. Pull up tightly and secure. Make a pompon (*see* Techniques page 13) in main color and attach to top of hat.

PADDINGTON BEAR'S DUFFLE COAT

Materials
Wendy Ascot Chunky –
red (426): 350/350/350/
1,000gm; black: 50/50/50/
100gm; blue (398), yellow
(399), dark brown (13) and
nut brown (11): 50gm of
each. 3/3/3/4 1¾in toggles
for front; 2 1¼in toggles
for motif on back.

Needles
One pair of No.10
needles.

Gauge
Using No.10 needles and
measured over st st, 14 sts
and 20 rows = 4in square.

A chunky-weight duffle coat that is suitable
for all the family. It is worked using the
intarsia method (*see* Techniques, page 8).

Back
Using No.10 needles and red, cast on 52/57/
61/94 sts. Work in k2, p2 rib for 1in, then

The chart opposite
should be followed for
the back of the adult's
coat. The crosses indicate
where the toggles and
toggle cords should be
fixed, and the dotted line
indicates the line of chain
stitch, which should be
embroidered in light
brown.

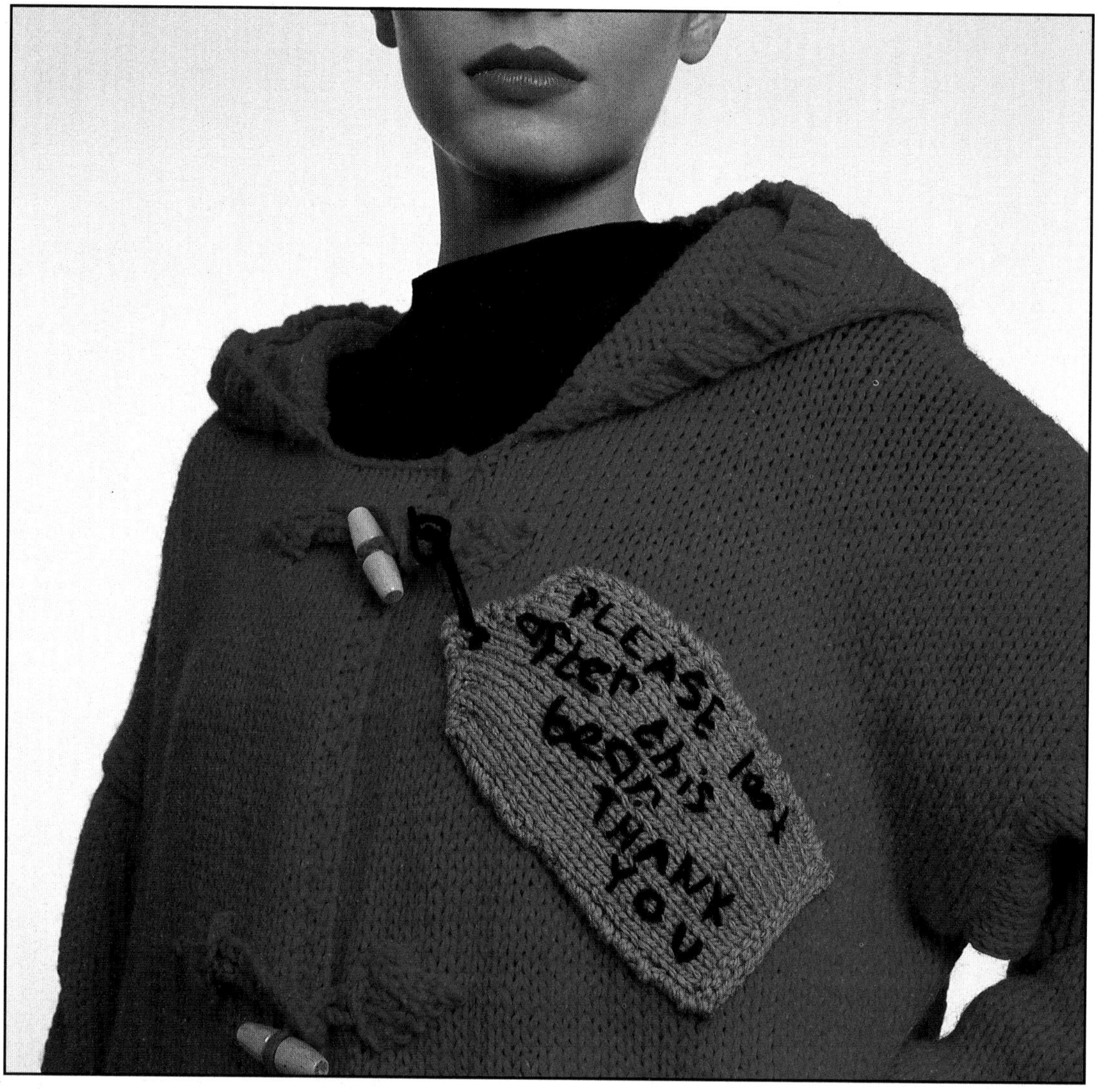

PLEASE look
after this
bear
THANK
YOU

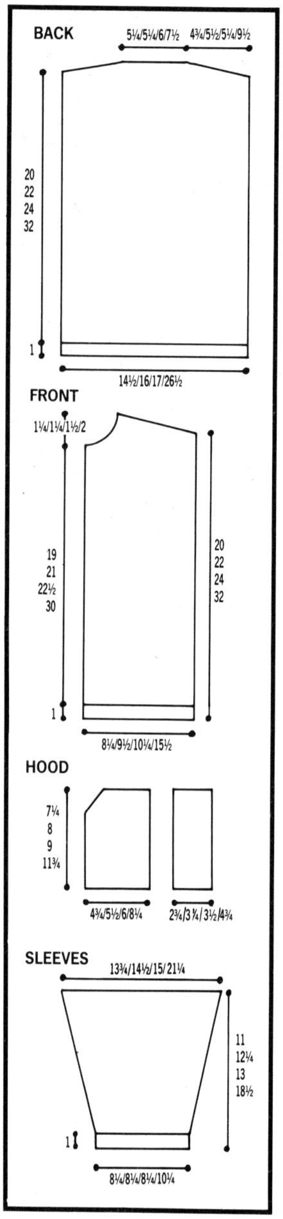

BACK
5¼/5¼/6/7½
4¾/5½/5¼/9½
20
22
24
32
1
14½/16/17/26½
FRONT
1¼/1¼/1½/2
19
21
22½
30
20
22
24
32
1
8¼/9½/10¼/15½
HOOD
7¼
8
9
11¾
4¾/5½/6/8¼
2¾/3¼/3½/4¾
SLEEVES
13¾/14½/15/21¼
11
12¼
13
18½
1
8¼/8¾/8¾/10¼

cont in st st starting with a k row for 10/16/24/12 rows. Working the small chart for the first three sizes and the large chart for the fourth size, establishing pattern as follows: k3/6/8/8 sts. Work first row of appropriate chart, k to end. Next row: p3/5/7/7 sts. Work second row of chart, cont in st st, working chart as placed until it is complete. Cont to work even in main color only until work measures 20/22/24/32in, ending with a WS row. Bind off 8/9/10/11 sts at beg of the next 2 rows. Bind off 9/10/10/11 sts at beg of the next 2 rows. **Large size only:** bind off 11 sts at beg of the next 2 rows. **All sizes:** bind off remaining 18/19/21/28 sts.

Left front
Cast on 30/33/36/54 sts in red and work in k2, p2 rib for 1in. Now cont in st st with front edge border as follows:
RS rows: knit to last st, k1, k1b.
WS rows: sl 1, k2, purl to end.

This will give a neat front edge to jacket. Repeat these 2 rows until work measures 19/21/22½/30in, ending at front edge.
Shape neck: bind off 7/7/7/12 sts at beg of the next row, work to end, work 1 row, now dec 1 st at neck edge on every row until 17/19/20/33 sts remain. Cont in st st until work measures same as back to shoulder, ending with RS of work facing. **Shape shoulder:** bind off 8/9/10/11 sts at beg of the next row, work 1 row, bind off 9/10/10/11 sts at beg of the next row. **Adult size only:** work 1 row. Bind off remaining sts.

Right front
Work as for the left front, reversing all the shapings.

Sleeves (Make 2)
Cast on 30/30/30/36 sts in red and work in k2, p2 rib for 1in. Now work in st st, inc 1 st at each end of every following 5th/5th/5th/4th

rows until there are 50/52/54/76 sts. Cont in
st st until work measures 11/12¼/13/18½in.
Bind off all sts.

Patch pockets (Make 2)

Cast on 14/16/18/20 sts in red and work in
st st for 4/4¼/4¾/6in. Now work in k2, p2 rib
for 1in. Bind off in ribbing.

Hood (Side sections: work 2)

Cast on 17/20/21/30 sts in red and work in
st st until work measures 5¼/6¼/6¾/9in,
ending at front edge.
Next row: knit.
Next row: sl 1, p 2 sts together, p to end.
Repeat these 2 rows until 13/15/17/24 sts
remain, then cont in st st until work
measures 7¼/8/9/11¾in. Bind off all sts.

Center back section

Cast on 10/11/12/16 sts in red and work in
st st until back section fits neatly along
shaped edge of side section. Bind off all sts.
Sew center back section to shaped edges of
side sections to form hood.

Edging

Using red and RS of work facing, pick up
and knit approximately 72/82/102/120 sts
evenly around front of hood. Work in k2, p2
rib for 1in. Bind off in ribbing.

Toggle holders

Cast on 6/6/6/8 sts in red and work in st st,
dec 1 st at beg of every row (dec inside edge
stitch to give a neat edge) until 2 sts remain.
Work 1 row, then work remaining 2 sts tog
and fasten off. Work 5/5/5/7 more toggle
holders to match.

Toggle cords

Cast on 2 sts in red. Work in st st to make a
cord 3¼in long, fasten off. Work 2/2/2/3
more. Using blue wool, cast on 2 sts. Work
in st st to make a cord 1½in long. Bind off,
work 1/1/1/1 more. Using red wool, make a
single chain 2¼in long. Work 2/2/2/3 more.

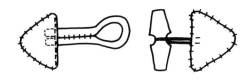

Label

Cast on 2 sts. K 1 row, inc 1 st at each end of
the next row, the 3 following alt rows and
the 3 following rows (14 sts). Work even for

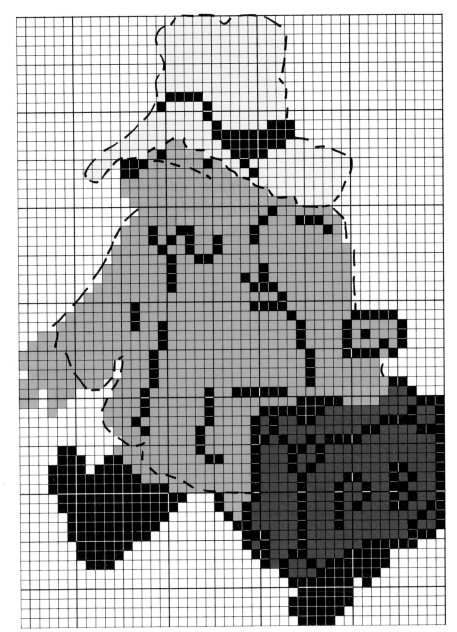

Incorporate this chart into
the child's duffle coat.
Outline the hat, coat and
snout in chain stitch,
following the dotted
lines, using yellow for the
hat, blue for the coat and
light brown for the snout.

29 rows. Next row (WS): knit. Bind off. Using black wool, embroider "Please look after this bear. Thank you", as shown on the diagram.

Finishing

Join shoulder seam. Set in sleeves, sew in place. Sew pockets into position on fronts setting at top of rib in place as desired. Join side and sleeve seams using a flat seam. Pin toggle holders into position with the long edge facing the inner bands. Sew side edges in place. Fold red toggle cords in half, tuck into holders and stitch down firmly. Tie narrow toggle cord around toggle and sew ends into opposite holders.

Sew blue toggle cords onto Paddington's coat, secure toggles to other side with a double strand of wool.

Using chain st, outline the hat and coat on smaller sizes (*see* Techniques, page 12) as indicated on the small chart.

HUG ME DRESS

A huge "huggable" fluffy teddy dress with dolman sleeves. Easy to knit, it is worked in one piece using the intarsia method (*see* Techniques, page 8).

Dress

Using No.9 needles and peacock, cast on 64 sts. Work in k1, p1 rib for 8¾in, inc 8 sts evenly across the last row of rib (72 sts).

Change to No.10 needles and, starting with a knit row, begin following chart in st st, inc 1 st at each end of every alt row until you have 170 sts. Cont to work even following chart for another 24 rows.

Shape neck: next row (RS): k63, leave remaining sts on a spare needle and working on this first set of sts only, p 1 row. Dec 1 st at neck edge on next row and the next 2 alt

Materials

Wendy Soft Touch – peacock (58): 550gm; rose (59), yellow (55), white (54) and black (65): less than 50gm of each. 2 googly eyes 1in in diameter.

Needles

One pair of No.9 and one pair of No.10 needles.

Gauge

Using No.10 needles and measured over st st, 16 sts and 18 rows = 4in square.

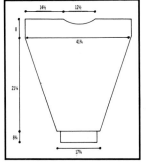

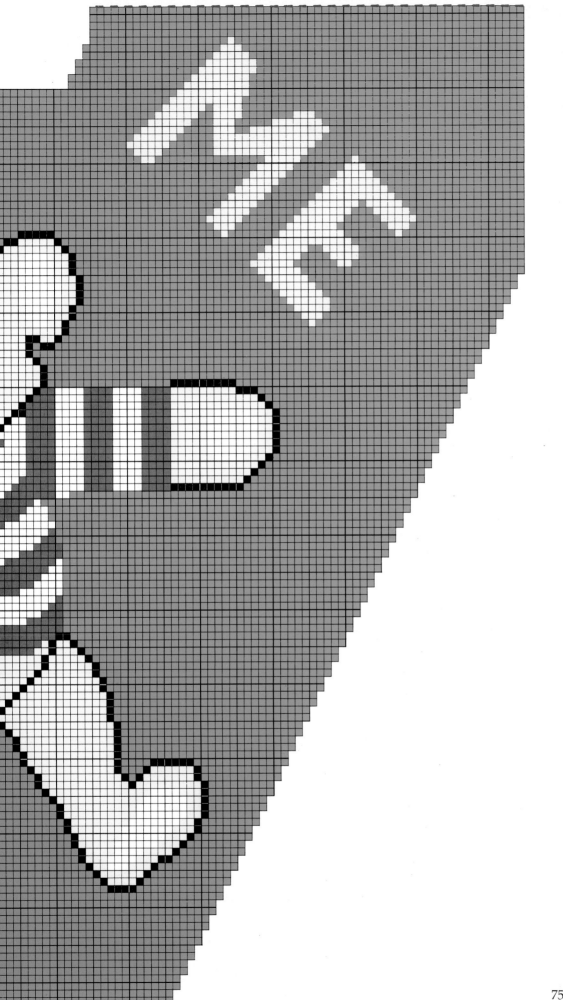

Follow this chart to complete the front of the sweater. The black dotted line indicates where teddy's mouth should be embroidered in running stitch; the red dotted line indicates the fold; and the crosses indicate where you should attach the bear's eyes.

rows, work 4 rows even, inc 1 st at neck edge on next row and the next 3 alt rows. Leave sts on a spare needle and rejoin yarn to center front. Bind off 44 sts, k to end. P 1 row. Dec 1 st at neck edge on next row and the 3 following alt rows. Work 4 rows. Inc 1 st at neck edge on next row and the next 3 alt rows. P across the 63 sts. Cast on 44 sts for center back. P across the 63 sts held for other side of neck. Cont in main color only, work 24 rows even, then dec 1 st at each end of the next row and every alt row until you have 72 sts.

Change to No.9 needles and work in k1, p1 rib for 8¾in. Bind off loosely in ribbing.

Collar

Using No.10 needles, cast on 100 sts. Work in k1, p1 rib for 8¾in. Bind off very loosely in ribbing.

Cuffs

Using No.9 needles, cast on 36 sts. Work in k1, p1 rib for 4 rows, then cont in rib, inc 1 st at each end of every alt row until you have 72 sts. Bind off.

Finishing

Join side seams and cuff seams using a flat seam. Join the short ends of the collar with an invisible seam. Stitch cuffs into place (with the wide end against the sleeve). Sew collar around the neck, keeping the seam at the center back of sweater. Embroider mouth using running stitch. Attach eyes.

BIG BEAR

A classic bear made using the traditional toymaking techniques. Big Bear is approximately 22¾in high when seated.

Instructions

All the pieces are worked using st st throughout, the knit side being the right side of your work. Each piece should be knitted separately and shaped by increasing and decreasing as indicated on each individual chart. Shapings should always be made on the second stitch and the stitch before the last stitch of every row and not on the very edge of the pieces. To increase, simply knit in the front and back of the stitch and to decrease, knit or purl two together according to whether you are working on the right side or wrong side of your work. Always work in the direction indicated by the arrow. To save confusion, label each piece as it is completed with the correct name on each part.
Work charts as follows:
Head side: knit 2 pieces (one reversed).
Body back: knit 2 pieces (one reversed).

Materials
Wendy Soft Touch – sable (62): 600gm. Wendy Aran – antelope (516): 50gm. Scraps of black wool. 3½lbs of polyester stuffing. One pair amber glass eyes; one plastic nose.

Needles
One pair of No.8 needles.

Gauge
Using No.8 needles and measured over st st, 18 sts and 24 rows = 4in square.

The charts on this page
and on pages 79, 80 and
81 should be worked
separately. The letter A
indicates that you should
use a lighter shade of
brown for these pieces;
the letter B indicates that
a darker shade should be
used to complete the foot
pads and paw pads.

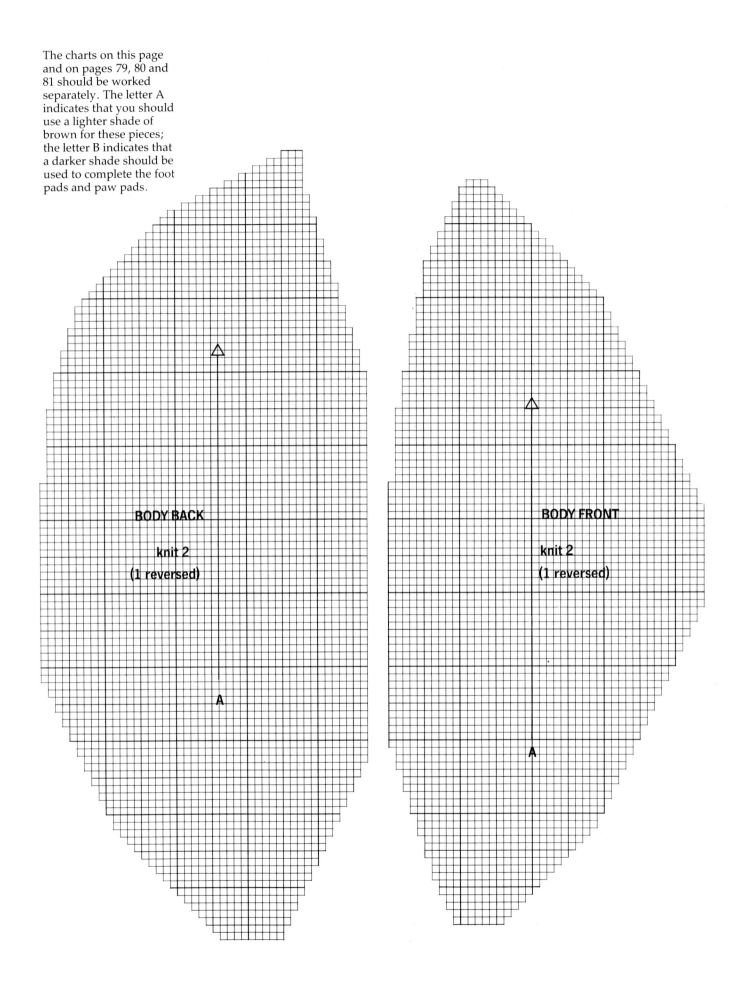

BODY BACK

knit 2

(1 reversed)

A

BODY FRONT

knit 2

(1 reversed)

A

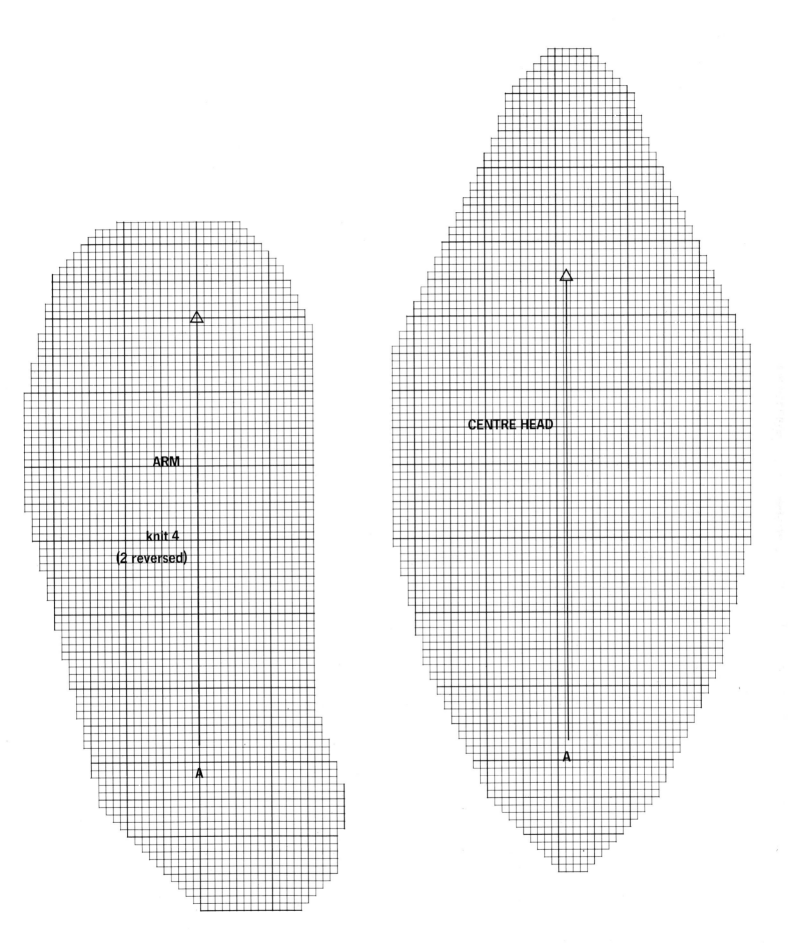

ARM

knit 4
(2 reversed)

A

CENTRE HEAD

A

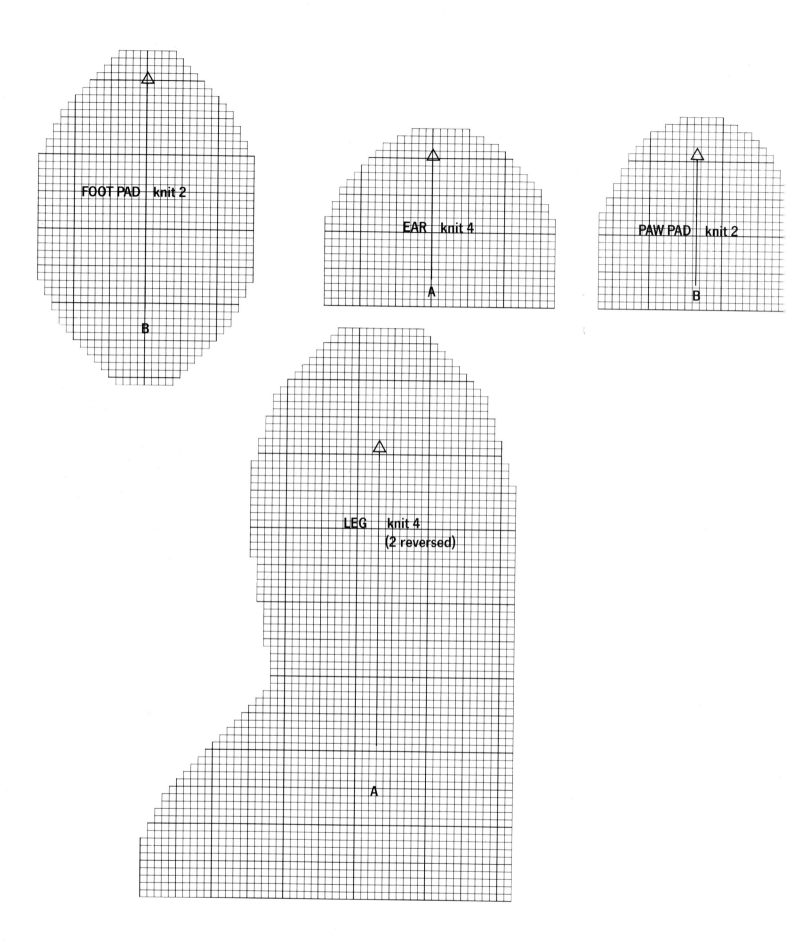

FOOT PAD   knit 2

B

EAR   knit 4

A

PAW PAD   knit 2

B

LEG   knit 4
(2 reversed)

A

Body front: knit 2 pieces (one reversed).
Arm: knit 4 pieces (2 reversed).
Leg: knit 4 pieces (2 reversed).
Center head: knit 1 piece.
Ear: knit 4 pieces.
Paw pad: knit 2 in brown.
Foot pad: knit 2 in brown.

Finishing

All seams should be narrow and worked with an overcast stitch.

Arms

Sew the paw pads curve to curve about 1in in from the bottom of the inner arms. With RS together, sew the inner armpiece to the outer armpiece leaving the shoulder end open and stuff firmly.

Legs

With RS of work together, stitch up the side seams of the outer and inner legs, leaving an opening at the top for stuffing and an opening at the bottom for the footpads. Stitch the footpads into position. Stuff the legs firmly, adding extra stuffing to thigh areas.

Body

Sew each front piece to back piece. This will form seams that run up the bear's sides. Now carefully stitch the two halves of the body together forming seams that run up teddy's tummy and back, leaving an opening at the back for stuffing. Stuff firmly and sew up opening.

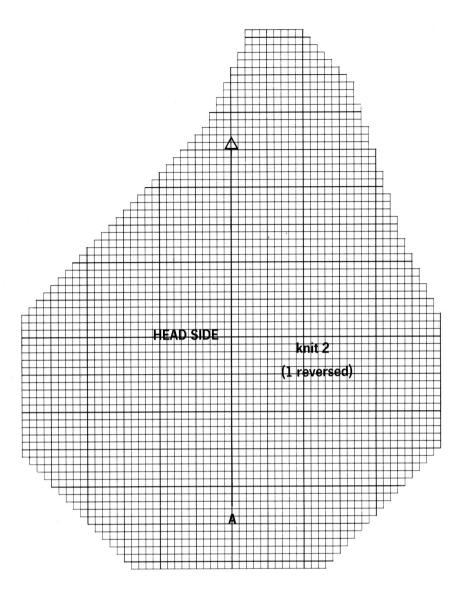

HEAD SIDE

knit 2
(1 reversed)

A

Head

Take the two head sides and, with RS together, sew up from the neck opening to the top of the snout. Then sew on the head center, starting from the back of the neck opening and stitching right around to the nose and back down the other side to the neck opening. Turn work right side out and stuff. Attach nose to top point of snout and embroider on mouth using one vertical and one horizontal stitch. Place eyes in position (to the desired expression) and fix firmly. Place head on top of body and tack into position, adding extra stuffing to keep neck firm. Tack arm-tops and leg-tops to body, placing them in a sitting position and stuffing firmly as you go. Using mohair, overcast all pieces into position as tacked, working twice round each piece to ensure they are secure.

Ears

Place two earpieces RS together and sew around curved edge. Turn RS out and, using a small backstitch, sew a line about ½in in from the curve to form a ridge at the top. Sew bottom edge together, gathering slightly as you go. Pin into position using the photograph as reference and sew firmly into position. Repeat for other ear.

KID'S SQUEAKY SWEATER

Materials
Wendy Family Choice DK wool – chilled cream or valentine: 250/300/300/350gm; blue (216) and yellow (267): 50gm of each. A scrap of black yarn. A small amount of polyester batting. One flat plastic squeaker.

Needles
One pair of No.4 and one pair of No.6 needles.

Gauge
Using No.6 needles and measured over st st, 24 sts and 32 rows = 4in square.

A bright sweater decorated with an appliqué teddy that squeaks. You can personalize this sweater by Swiss darning a child's name using our lettering chart. Knitted in stockinette stitch, the sweater will fit children aged 2–3, 3–4, 5–6 and 7–8 years.

Personalize the sweater by using Swiss darning (*see* page 13) to embroider a child's name on it. Select the appropriate letters from the chart opposite.

Front

** Using No.4 needles, cast on 76/84/88/96 sts.

Row 1: k1, *k2, p2, rep from * to last 3 sts, k3.

Row 2: k1, *p2, k2, rep from * to last 3 sts, p2, k1.

Repeat these last 2 rows until work measures 2in, ending with a first row. Inc 3/1/3/1 sts evenly across next row (78/85/91/97 sts). Change to No.6 needles.** Work in st st for 94/100/116/130 rows. **Shape neck:** next row: k28/31/34/36, turn. Cont to work on this set of sts as follows: dec 1 st at beg of the next row.*** Dec 1 st at neck edge on the next and every following alt row until 24/26/29/31 sts remain. Work 5/5/7/7 rows even, finishing on a WS row.

Shape shoulder: bind off remaining sts.***
With RS of work facing, rejoin yarn to remaining 48/51/55/58 sts. Next row: k17/17/19/19 sts. Slip these sts onto a stitch holder. K to end. Cont working on the last 31/34/36/39 sts as follows: dec 1 st at the end of the next row. Work from *** to ***.

Back

Work as for front from ** to **. Cont working in st st until back measures the same as front to shoulder, finishing on a WS row. **Shape shoulders:** next row: bind off 24/26/29/31 sts. K31/33/33/35 sts. Bind off remaining 24/26/29/31 sts. Slip center 31/33/33/35 sts onto a stitch holder. Break off yarn.

Sleeves (Make 2)

Using No.4 needles, cast on 40/44/44/44 sts. Work 2in in rib as for front, finishing on a WS row.

Change to No.6 needles and work in st st, inc 1 st at each end of the next and every following second row for the first three sizes (every following fourth row for the fourth size), until you have 50/50/50/92 sts, then on every following 4th/4th/4th/6th row until you have 78/84/90/96 sts. Cont to work even until sleeve measures 11½/13/14½/17in (including rib), finishing on a WS row. Bind off loosely. Join left shoulder seam.

Neckband

With RS of work facing and using No.4 needles, k31/33/33/35 sts from back neck stitch holder. Pick up and k16/17/18/19 sts down left side of neck. K17/17/19/19 sts from front neck stitch holder and pick up 16/17/18/19 sts up RS of neck (80/84/88/92 sts).

Beginning with a second row, work in rib as for front for 8 rows. K 1 row. Work 10 more rows in rib. Bind off loosely in ribbing. Join right shoulder seam, join neckband seam and slip stitch bound-off edge of neckband to pick-up edge.

Finishing

Join sleeves to sweater using a narrow backstitch. Join sleeve and side seams using flat seams throughout.

Inside pocket

Using No.6 needles and main color, cast on 20 sts. Work in st st until work measures 3¼in. Bind off.

MOTIFS

Teddy

Beginning with the legs, using No.4 needles and yellow yarn used double, cast on 6 sts. K 4 rows. Bind off 3 sts at beg of the next

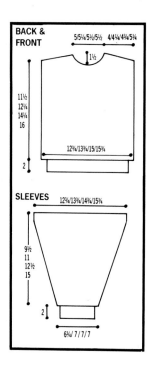

row. Inc 1 st at each end of the next row (5 sts). K 7 rows. Break off yarn, slip these sts onto a spare needle. Work second leg as for first, but work 6 rows instead of 7. Knit across the 10 sts from both legs, k 10 rows. Cast on 8 sts at beg of the next 2 rows, k 4 rows, dec 1 st at each end of the next row. Bind off 9 sts at the beg of the following 2 rows (6 sts). K 1 row. Inc 1 st at each end of the next row (8 sts). K 9 rows. Inc 1 st at each end of the next row (10 sts).

Shape ears next row: k5, turn, k3, k2 tog, turn, k2 tog. K2, turn, bind off 3 sts. Fasten off. Rejoin yarn at inner edge k3, k2 tog, turn, k2 tog, k2, turn. Bind off 3 sts. Fasten off.

Kite
Using No.4 needles and red, cast on 2 sts. K 1 row, inc 1 st at each end of the next row, the following 4th row and the four following 5th rows. K 1 row, dec 1 st at each end of the

next row and the 4 following alt rows (4 sts). Next row: k2 tog, knit last 2 sts together, fasten off.

Small bow (Make 2)

Using No.4 needles and blue wool used double, cast on 4 sts. K 3 rows, k2 tog, k2 tog, k 2 rows, inc 1 st at each end of the next row, k 2 rows. Bind off.

Bow-tie

Using No.4 needles and blue wool used double, cast on 10 sts. K 3 rows, dec 1 st at each end of the next row, the following 4th row and the following alt row, k 10 rows. Inc 1 st at each end of the next row, the following alt row and the following 4th row. K 3 rows. Bind off.

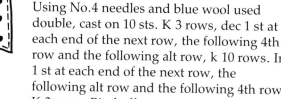

Sewing on the motifs

Pin the teddy motif on the front of the sweater, placing it at an angle on the bottom corner. Leaving ears, paws and feet free, stitch as illustrated on the diagram and stuff the legs, arms, head and tummy. Wind blue yarn several times around the center of a small bow and stitch below teddy's chin. Sew kite into position in the opposite top corner. With black wool, make one horizontal stitch across the kite and one stitch from top to bottom. Arrange a curling trail of black wool from the kite to teddy's paw and stitch into position. Sew a small bow just before end of trail. Embroider teddy's face as positioned on diagram.

Bow-tie: fold the bow-tie in half, RS together, and join just before the increasing starts. Stitch bow to center front neck just below the neck rib. Using red wool, make small knots on the bow for spots.

Inside pocket: position pocket so that the bottom edge is level with the bottom of teddy's tummy. Using running stitch, join to inside of sweater leaving a top opening and insert plastic squeaker.

NOTE: Remember to remove the squeaker before washing the sweater.

TEDDY BASEBALL JACKET

A sporty jacket worked in an aran-weight yarn using the intarsia method (*see* Techniques, page 8).

Left front
** Using No.5 needles and yellow, cast on 51 sts.

Materials
Wendy Action Knit – green (514): 500gm; yellow (539): 150gm; red (527): 50gm; black (530): 50gm; white (510) and blue (513): less than 50gm of each. Ascot DK wool used double – amber (412): less than 50gm. 8 buttons, ½in in diameter.

Needles
One pair of No.5 and one pair of No.7 needles.

Gauge
Using No.7 needles and measured over st st, 19 sts and 24 rows = 4in square.

The chart overleaf should be followed to complete the back of the jacket (*see* page 90). The chart on page 90 should be incorporated into the left front.

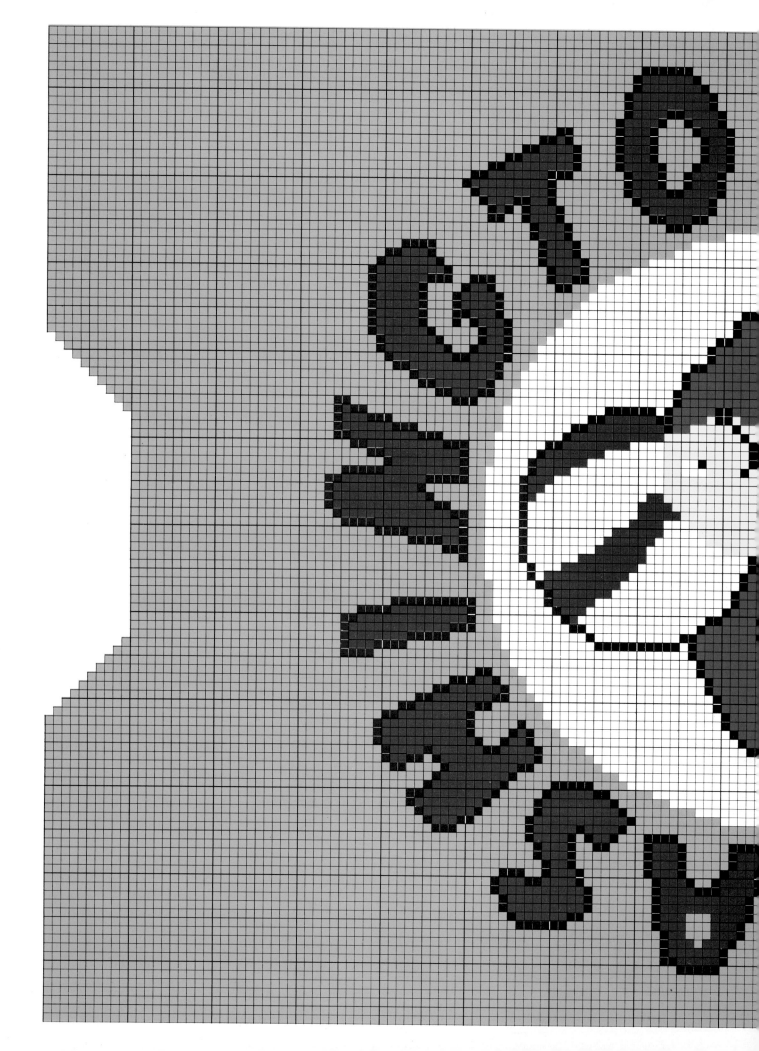

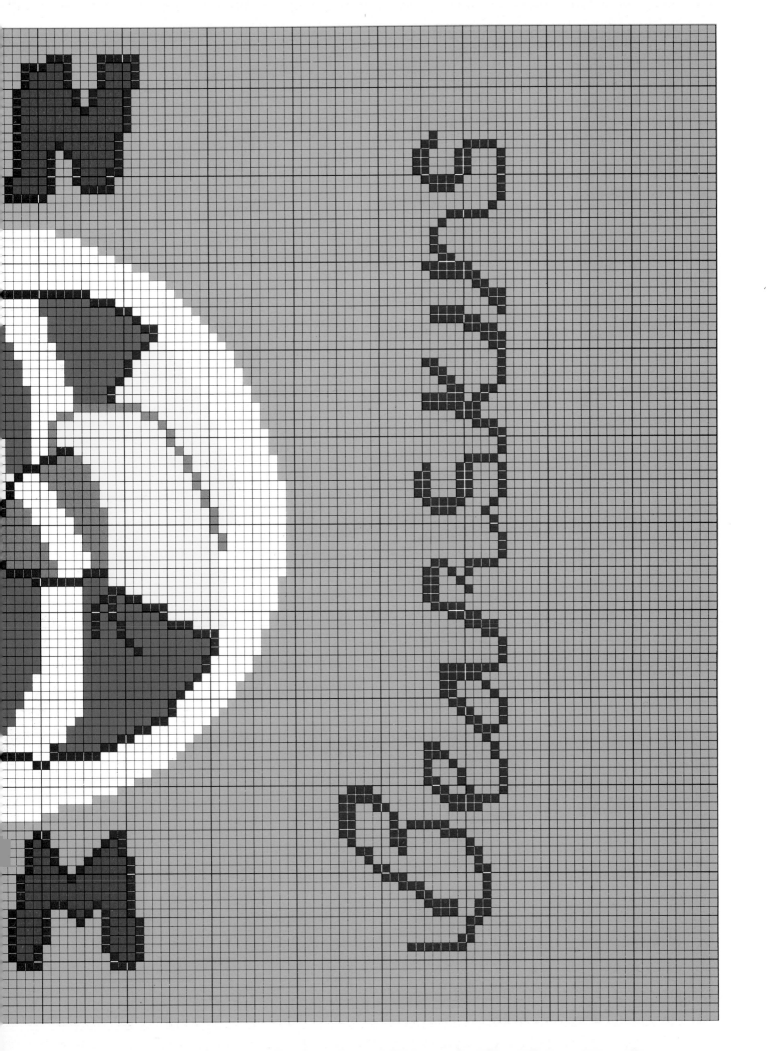

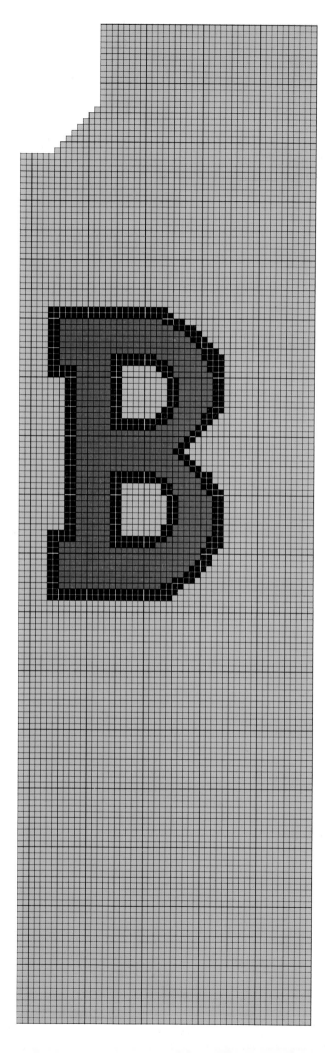

Row 1: k1, *p1, k1, rep from * to end.
Row 2: p1, *k1, p1, rep from * to end.
Row 3: work as for row 1.
Row 4: with green, purl.
Rows 5–8: with green, repeat rows 1 and 2 twice.
Row 9: with yellow, knit.
Row 10: with yellow, work as for row 2.
Rows 11 and 12: with yellow, repeat rows 1 and 2 once.
Row 13: with green, knit.
Row 14: with green, work as for row 2.
Rows 15–20: with green, repeat rows 1 and 2 three times.
Row 21: with green, work as for row 1.
Row 22: work as row 2 but inc into last stitch (52 sts).
Change to No.7 needles and begin following the chart, working in st st to neck shaping: next row: bind off 6 sts, p to end. Dec 1 st at neck edge on every row until 38 sts remain. Work 14 rows more in st st. Bind off.

Right front
Work as for left front, but reverse shaping and eliminate motif.

Back
Using No.5 needles and yellow, cast on 107 sts. Work the 21 rows of rib as for front.
Row 22: inc 7 sts evenly across row (114 sts).
Change to No.7 needles and begin working in st st, following chart to neck shaping.
Shape neck: work 44 sts, slip remaining sts onto a spare needle and, working on this side only, dec 1 st at neck edge on every row for 9 rows. Work 1 row. Bind off. Rejoin yarn to remaining sts. Bind off center 26 sts, work to end. Repeat shaping as for other side of neck. Bind off.

Sleeves (Make 2)
Using No.5 needles and yellow, cast on 43 sts. Work the 21 rows of rib as for front and inc 12 sts evenly across the 22nd row (55 sts).
Change to No.7 needles and begin following the sleeve chart, working in st st.

Pocket linings (Make 2)
Using No.7 needles and green, cast on 33 sts. Work 6¾in in st st, finishing on a WS row. Bind off.
Join shoulder seams.

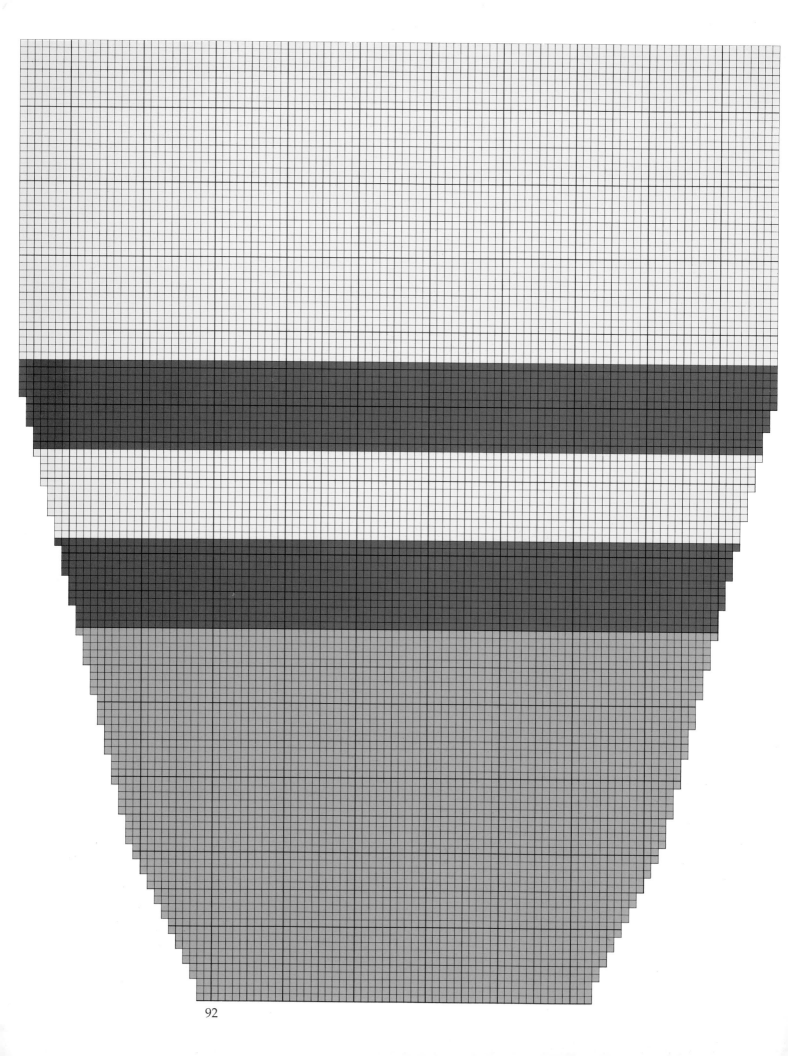

Follow the chart opposite
to complete both sleeves.

BACK

7   9½

28

3½

23½

FRONT

8

3½

28

3½

10½

SLEEVES

21¼

21¼

3½

11½

Neckband

Using No.5 needles, green and with RS facing, pick up and k 22 sts up right front neck, 8 sts down right back neck, 26 sts across back neck, 8 sts up left back neck and 23 sts down left front neck (87 sts).
Row 1: p1, *k1, p1, rep from * to end.
Row 2: k1, *p1, k1, rep from * to end.
Row 3: work as for row 1.
Row 4: with yellow, knit.
Rows 5 and 6: with yellow, repeat rows 1 and 2.
Row 7: with green, purl.
Row 8: with green, work as for row 2.
Rows 9 and 10: with green, repeat rows 1 and 2.
Row 11: with green, repeat row 1.
Row 12: with yellow, knit.
Rows 13 and 14: with yellow, repeat rows 1 and 2.
Row 15: with green, purl.
Using green only and beginning on a second row, work 14 more rows in rib. Bind off in ribbing. Fold neckband in half to wrong side and slip stitch bound-off edge to pick-up edge.

Buttonband

Using No.5 needles, green, and with RS facing, starting at the top of the neckband, pick up and k 145 sts evenly down left front to lower edge. Work the first 13 rows of rib as given for neckband. With yellow, bind off in ribbing.

Buttonhole band

Using No.5 needles, green, and RS facing, starting at the lower edge, pick up and k 145 sts evenly up right front to top of neckband. Work the first 7 rows of rib as given for neckband. Next row (make buttonholes): rib 5, *yrn, dec 1 st, rib 17, rep from * to last 7 sts, yrn, dec 1 st, rib to end. Beginning on the 9th row, work 5 more rows in rib as given for neckband. Using yellow, bind off in rib. For a man's jacket, reverse the positions of the button and buttonhole bands.

Finishing

Join side seams with a narrow backstitch, leaving 6¾in open above the rib for the pocket linings. **Make pocket edgings:** using No.5 needles, green and RS facing, pick up and k 39 sts evenly along open edge of front side seam. Work the first 13 rows of rib as given for neckband. With yellow, bind off in ribbing.
Join the edge of the pocket linings to the back side seam with an invisible seam. Slip stitch pocket linings to fronts to make pocket.
Sew sleeves into position and join sleeve seams.
Sew on buttons.

YARN INFORMATION

All the sample garments illustrated in this book were knitted in Wendy yarns. If you have trouble finding Wendy Wools in your area, contact:

Berroco Inc.
Elmdale Road
P.O. Box 367
Uxbridge
Massachusetts 01569

As many of the designs contain small quantities of several different colors, Melinda Coss offers individual kits containing only the quantities of Wendy yarn necessary to complete each garment. In addition, buttons, embroidery threads and trimmings are included where appropriate.
Contact Melinda Coss at 1 Copenhagen Street, London N1 0JB, UK (telephone 01-833 3929). The kits are available by mail order only.

For those who wish to substitute different yarns, weights are given throughout to the nearest 50gm ball. To obtain the best results, you must ensure that the gauge recommended on your selected yarn matches the gauge printed in our pattern. We cannot guarantee your results if this rule is not followed.